# THE OSSLT LITERACY LAB

## Answer Key and Teacher's Guide

# THE OSSLT LITERACY LAB

## Answer Key and Teacher's Guide

ĕß

echo
BOOKS

An imprint of
Wintertickle PRESS

Acknowledgement: A special thank you goes out to all the teachers and consultants who contributed to this project with their suggestions, proof-reading and invaluable input.

Photo and writing credits can be found throughout the book. If no credit is attributed within the text, the writing is credited to H.A. Fraser and the stock photos are credited to iStockphoto or Dreamstime. All written material, illustrations and photos have been granted permission or are licensed for use in this resource. For information, please contact the publisher directly.

Disclaimer: Wintertickle Press endeavours to have up-to-date information regarding the Ontario Secondary School Literacy Test (OSSLT) at the time of publication. However, this information changes often. For details on the specifics of the OSSLT, please check with the Educational Quality and Accountability Office (EQAO) website. Wintertickle Press does not warrant the information about the OSSLT in this book to be accurate. This publication is for literacy educational purposes only and does not guarantee a student will pass the OSSLT.

Published and distributed by:

Wintertickle **PRESS**

132 Commerce Park Drive, Unit K, Suite 155
Barrie, ON, L4N 0Z7

ĕß
e c h o
BOOKS

OSSLTLiteracyLab.com
WintertticklePress.com

Printed and bound in Canada

ISBN 978-1-894813-72-3

# Acknowledgements

A heartfelt acknowledgement of appreciation goes out to the many educators who graciously donated their time and expertise to this project. Without their input, reviews and feedback, this project would not exist. Thank you goes out to:

Candice Allen, Greater Essex County District School Board

Lisa Beganyi, Peterborough Victoria Northumberland Clarington Catholic District School Board

Liana Blaskievich, Near North District School Board

Christine Cammaert, London District Catholic School Board

James Chambers, Dufferin-Peel Catholic District School Board

Francesca Cioffi, York Region District School Board

Lindsay Duwyn, Brant Haldimand Norfolk Catholic District School Board

Rachel Cranswick, Toronto District School Board

Pamela Crawford, Bluewater District School Board

Anita De Oliveira, Toronto District School Board

Antonio Della Ventura, Niagara Catholic District School Board

Paula Diamond, Dufferin-Peel Catholic District School Board

Jessica Folino, District School Board of Niagara

Anne-Marie Fraser, Ottawa Catholic School Board

Hillary Gallivan, London District Catholic School Board

Sean Gallivan, London District Catholic School Board

Barbara Ginn, Kawartha Pine Ridge District School Board

Brian Goodram, Hamilton-Wentworth District School Board

Kelly Griffiths, Keewatin-Patricia District School Board

Christina Groppo, Hamilton-Wentworth Catholic District School Board

Linda Hancox, Kawartha Pine Ridge District School Board

Laurie Hayden, Avon Maitland District School Board

Kathleen Jarvis, London District Catholic School Board

Bonnie Jefford, Windsor-Essex Catholic District School Board

Pam Jeffrey, Simcoe County District School Board

Stephanie Jolley, Near North District School Board

Penta Ledger, Trillium Lakelands District School Board

Kim Leenhuis, Ottawa-Carleton District School Board

Linda Luffman, Peel District School Board

Phyllis MacLeod, Waterloo Region District School Board

Rick MacMillan, Greater Essex County District School Board

Joanne Mantha McConnell, Huron-Superior Catholic District School Board

Jordan Matteis, St. Clair Catholic District School Board

Gillian Maxwell, Durham District School Board

Janet Maxwell, Toronto District School Board

Robynn McFadden, Peterborough Victoria Northumberland Clarington Catholic District School Board

David McKillop, York Region District School Board

Jane Mitchinson-Schwartz, Waterloo Region District School Board

Kimberly Mockler, London District Catholic School Board

Diane Moser, Waterloo Region District School Board

Karen Murray, London District Catholic School Board

Melissa Nicholls, Durham District School Board

Michelle Noble, Kawartha Pine Ridge District School Board

Vincent O'Brien, Simcoe Muskoka Catholic District School Board

Rachael Proulx, Hamilton-Wentworth District School Board

Karla Queckenstedt, Grand Erie District School Board

Karen Quesnel, Simcoe County District School Board

Narda Robbins, Thames Valley District School Board

Jennifer Skeggs, Thames Valley District School Board

Amy Stokes, Peel District School Board

Laura Stringer, Rainbow District School Board

Vanessa Swance, Upper Grand District School Board

Holly Szumowski, Keewatin-Patricia District School Board

Vanessa Taylor, Trillium Lakelands District School Board

MJ Thexton, Toronto District School Board

Amelia Thompson, Peterborough Victoria Northumberland Clarington Catholic District School Board

Sonya Valente, Near North District School Board

Lianne Van De Wal, Nippising-Parry Sound Catholic District School Board

Stacey Walsh, Nippising-Parry Sound Catholic District School Board

David Way, Ottawa-Carleton District School Board

Melanie White, Ottawa-Carleton District School Board

Jon Young, Algoma District School Board

**Additional editing and writing contributions graciously provided by:**

Lisa Beganyi

Michael McNeely

Fred Thomas

Jon Young

# Feedback

## "We're not perfect... but we'd like to be!"

Although a lot of care was taken with the production of this resource, mistakes happen—especially when working with a limited number of staff and a very tight deadline. So, if you notice something amiss, please do not let it fester and irritate you. Instead, please tell us! We want to know—and more importantly—we want to fix it. Please report any errors, omissions or misinformation to ontarioliteracylab@outlook.com.

## "We want to know what's going on!"

Knowing how our resource is being used interests us, and learning of your school's success is important to us. We like to hear good news too! Please send along any stories or comments to ontarioliteracylab@outlook.com. Or, if you have something good to say to the world, feel free to review the resource online at www.amazon.com or www.chapters.indigo.ca.

## "Are you right to write for us?"

We have so much in development, it is making our heads spin. Although that is a metaphor, it isn't far from reality. We are always on the lookout for great, wonderful educators like yourself to help develop resources that truly helps students achieve their potential. That is our mission statement and our primary focus. Everything else is secondary. Please fire us an email if you would like to be considered for future review committees or have a resource idea.

# Table of Contents

# SECTION 1

**THE OSSLT ANSWER LAB**

# **Answer Lab:** sample answers for the activities

. . . . . . . . . . . . . . . . . . . . . . . . . . . . . . . . . . . . . . . . . . . . . . . . . . . .

The Answer Lab is a copy of several sections of *The OSSLT Literacy Lab Student Workbook* with sample answers included. Just look for the corresponding page to the workbook found inside the border to see the answers. The written responses are examples of answers that would be awarded at least a pass on the test. You will also find the Student Answer Sheet for the sample test at the end of this section.

# SECTION 1

# Section 1: The OSSLT Reading Lab

The OSSLT assesses your skills through a variety of reading selections.

- **information paragraph:** presents ideas and information on a topic
- **news report:** presents information in the form of a news story
- **dialogue:** presents a conversation between two or more people
- **real-life narrative:** presents an account of a significant time in an individual's life
- **graphic text:** presents ideas and information with the help of graphic features, such as diagrams, photographs, drawings, sketches, patterns, timetables, maps, charts or tables

They vary in length from a single paragraph to two pages.

For the OSSLT, "reading" is the process through which you make meaning of a variety of written texts, focussing on three skills:

1. understanding explicitly (directly) stated ideas and information;
2. understanding implicitly (indirectly) stated ideas and information; and
3. making connections between information and ideas in a reading selection and personal knowledge and experience.

There are two types of questions in the reading components of the OSSLT:

- **multiple-choice:**
  Each reading text is followed by a number of multiple-choice questions. You are to select the best or most correct answer from a list of four options.

- **open-response:**
  The information paragraph, news report and dialogue are followed by one or two open-response questions. You are to construct a response based on the reading selection. **You should respond in the six lines provided in complete sentences.**

In this resource, you will be walked through two examples of each type of reading activity similar to those you will encounter on the OSSLT. You will find advice from fictional representations of typical Ontario students. Tips will be provided in the form of notes that are "paper-clipped" to your activities for ease of reference.

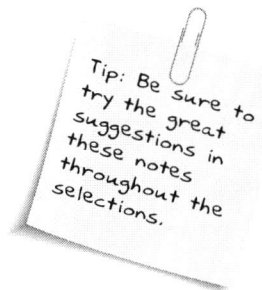

*Tip: Be sure to try the great suggestions in these notes throughout the selections.*

You will know you have not completed all the questions for a particular reading selection and will have to turn the page to continue if you see an arrow that says "Turn the page to complete this section."

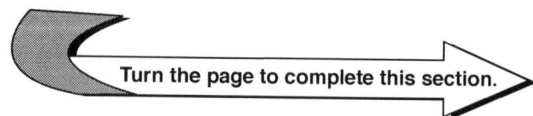

> **Turn the page to complete this section.**

You will know you have completed a section when you see the phrase "End of Section." in a grey rectangular box.

**End of Section.**

Information found on EQAO website. Check frequently for accuracy and updates.

# Information Paragraph: presents ideas and information on a particular topic

· · · · · · · · · · · · · · · · · · · · · · · · · · · · · · · · · · · · · · · · · · · · · · · · · · · ·

**Hi. My name is Marcus and I am from Nepean. The most difficult thing for me with information paragraphs is getting the main idea. I sometimes confuse the main idea with the topic. The topic refers to the subject of the paragraph, while the main idea deals with the point, thought or opinion being expressed in the paragraph. Here's a tip that really helped me. Give it a try. I always read the first and last sentences first. That gives me a strong idea of what the topic is. Then, I turn the first sentence into a question and read the paragraph to look for the answer. That helps me to figure out the main point. When I am done reading, I try to connect the information to things I already know. If I still have questions, I read the paragraph again.**

### Reading: Information Paragraph

**Read the selection below and answer the questions that follow it.**

*Tip: The numbers at the side of the selection indicate line numbers.*

Algonquin Provincial Park is an example of one location existing for a variety
of purposes. Established in 1893, it is the oldest provincial park in Canada. It is
approximately 7,653 square kilometres. In size, this is about one and a half times the
size of the province of Prince Edward Island. Because of its vast size and proximity
to major populated areas such as Ottawa and Toronto, Algonquin is one of the most          5
popular provincial parks in Canada. Algonquin Park is located between Georgian Bay
and the Ottawa River in Central Ontario, and an east-west road, Highway 60, runs right
through the south end of the park. Besides having over 2,400 lakes and 1,200 kilometres
of streams and rivers, Algonquin Provincial Park also has visitor interpretation
programmes, historic structures, camps, administration buildings and museums. The        10
park offers many different seasonal activities such as day hiking, camping, canoeing,
mountain biking, horseback riding and cross-country skiing. Interestingly, Algonquin
is the only designated park in Ontario to allow industrial logging to take place. Those
managing Algonquin Provincial Park work hard to balance tourism, conservation,
research and industry so its many purposes can exist in harmony all in one location.      15
Although Algonquin Park has been around for a long time, it is a gem that provides
enjoyment for its many yearly visitors.

*Tip: As you read, think about what you are reading and ask yourself questions about it.*

**Multiple-Choice** (Circle the best or most correct answer.)

**1** How large is Algonquin Provincial Park?

    **A** half the size of Prince Edward Island

    (**B**) one and a half times the size of Prince Edward Island

    **C** twice the size of Prince Edward Island

    **D** half the size of Quebec City

**2** Why is Algonquin Provincial Park popular with tourists?

    **A** It is extremely far from urban centres.

    **B** It has museums.

    (**C**) There are a lot of activities.

    **D** It is a small park.

**3** Which line demonstrates the use of commas to separate items in a list?

    **A** Line 2

    **B** Line 8

    (**C**) Line 11

    **D** Line 15

**4** Which of the following is closest in meaning to the word "gem" as used in line 16?

    (**A**) something special

    **B** precious stone

    **C** location with lots of rocks

    **D** jewellery

**5** What is the purpose of this selection?

    **A** to let readers know there is a lot to do at Algonquin Provincial Park

    **B** to provide facts on the size of the park

    **C** to describe the exact location of Algonquin Provincial Park

    (**D**) to explain that Algonquin Provincial Park serves many purposes

*Tip: Go back and read the word "gem" in context in the paragraph. The best answer is not the literal meaning of "gem."*

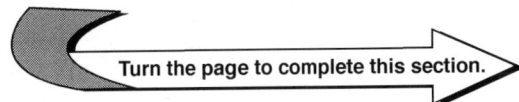

**Turn the page to complete this section.**

**Reading: Information Paragraph**

Hey. What's up? I am Zoe and my hometown is Tillsonburg. I find it really helpful to draw a graphic organizer so I can picture and organize the main points and details in information paragraphs that I read. I put the main idea in a circle in the centre, then I surround the main idea with satellite circles and write important information in them. In the OSSLT there is a spot called "Rough Notes." It isn't scored, but I use the space to create my graphic organizer. I suggest giving it a try below.

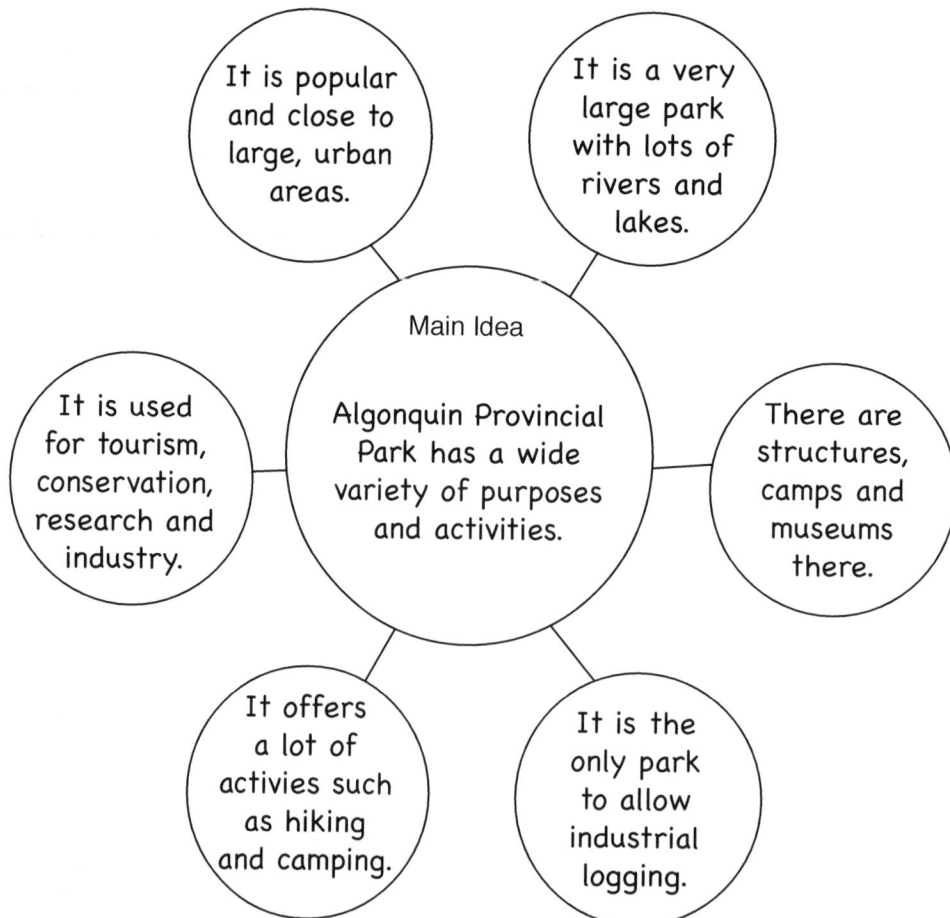

It is popular and close to large, urban areas.

It is a very large park with lots of rivers and lakes.

Main Idea

Algonquin Provincial Park has a wide variety of purposes and activities.

It is used for tourism, conservation, research and industry.

There are structures, camps and museums there.

It offers a lot of activies such as hiking and camping.

It is the only park to allow industrial logging.

12

**Reading: Information Paragraph**

**6** State a main idea of this selection and provide one specific detail from the selection that supports it.

Algonquin Provincial Park exists for a variety of many different

purposes. For example, Algonquin is a popular tourist

destination because of its many programs and activities

such as hiking and camping. In addition, industrial logging

is allowed at this location. Other purposes such as research and

conservation exist, making Algonquin Provincial Park a unique location.

*Tip: Remember the main idea is the point, thought or opinion—not simply the topic or what the piece was about.*

**7** Do you think Algonquin Provincial Park would be an interesting place to visit? Use information from the selection to support your answer.

*Tip: Here is a chance to draw upon your own experiences as well as use information from the paragraph.*

I think that Algonquin Provincial Park would be an interesting

place to visit. Not only is it a reasonable drive from my hometown

of Ottawa, but it offers my favourite activity, cross-country

skiing. In addition, I do enjoy going to museums and hiking.

Therefore, I would love the opportunity to visit the museum

there and try some of the day hiking available.

**Rough Notes**

*Use the space below for rough notes. Nothing you write in this space will be scored.*

*Tip: When you see "End of Section," you know you have come to the end of the questions for a particular activity.*

**End of Section.**

**Reading: Information Paragraph**

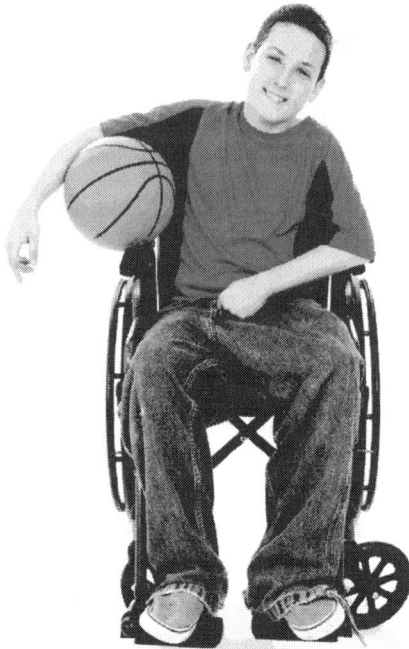

Hi there. I'm Carter and I live in Kenora. What I find challenging about information paragraphs is figuring out how they are organized. I look for transitional words or phrases to give me clues. Transitional words improve logical organization and make a paragraph easier to understand. They also improve the connections between thoughts. I underline transitional words and phrases when I read information paragraphs. Some common ways a paragraph can be organized are: chronological order, general to specific, cause and effect, and compare and contrast.

This chart provides examples of common transitional words and phrases, as well as what they express.

| Organization Type | Common Transitional Words |
|---|---|
| Chronological order | first, next, then, initially, before, after, when, finally, preceding, following |
| General to specific | for instance, for example, such as, to illustrate, a colon (:) followed by a list |
| Cause and effect | because of, as a result of, in order to, may be due to, effects of, therefore, consequently, for this reason, if, thus |
| Compare and contrast | different from, same as, similar to, as opposed to, instead of, although, however, compared with, as well as, either…or |

14

**Reading: Information Paragraph**

**Read the selection below and answer the questions that follow it.**

Ontario Northland Railway operates a Canadian passenger train called the Polar
Bear Express, which is the life-line connecting Cochrane and Moosonee. Initially,
this rail service was introduced back in 1964. There aren't any roads to Moosonee, so
supplies and people often come in and out by train. Although the official designation
for the Polar Bear Express is "passenger train," it also carries cargo such as canoes,     5
snowmobiles, all-terrain vehicles, cars and light trucks. The Polar Bear Express
currently operates five days per week year-round, and during the summer there are
additional trains added to the schedule. Before 2012, this train had a full dining car in
the summer months, but that has been discontinued. This Canadian passenger train
is not to be confused with the children's book by Chris Van Allsburg similarly named     10
*The Polar Express*. This vital service connecting these communities continues to be an
important part of Ontario's north.

Tip: Circle any transitional words you find in the paragraph to help you understand how it is organized.

Photo Credits: Kim Forster. Used with permission.

## Reading: Information Paragraph

**Multiple-Choice** (Circle the best or most correct answer.)

**1** Why is the Polar Bear Express considered a life-line to the people of Moosonee?

    **(A)** There are no roads leading to Moosonee.

    **B** It has a dining car providing food for the residents of Moosonee.

    **C** It is a passenger train.

    **D** It carries trucks to Moosonee.

**2** Which word is closest in meaning to "vital" as used in line 11?

    **A** optional

    **B** expendable

    **(C)** necessary

    **D** useful

**3** Why is "*The Polar Express*" italicized at the end of the paragraph?

    **A** to give emphasis

    **(B)** to indicate that it is a title of a book

    **C** to show that it is a train

    **D** to indicate that it is the end of the paragraph

**4** Why would the train run more often in the summer?

    **A** People eat more in the summer.

    **B** The weather is better.

    **C** There is a greater need for supplies in the summer.

    **(D)** There is more tourism in the summer.

**5** How are lines 5-6 grouped?

    **A** by the schedule

    **(B)** by what the train carries

    **C** by who uses the train

    **D** by the reasons the train exists

*Tip: Read all four answers before choosing one. You are looking for the best possible answer.*

**6** State a main idea of this selection and provide one specific detail from the selection that supports it.

The Polar Bear Express is a very important train for

Moosonee because there are no roads going into the town.

Not only does it carry passengers back and forth, but it

also shuttles important supplies such as canoes and vehicles.

Without this vital service, it would be extremely difficult for

people who live in Moosonee to get supplies.

*Tip: The number of lines gives you an indication of how much you should write.*

**Rough Notes**

*Use the space below for rough notes. Nothing you write in this space will be scored.*

*Tip: This is the perfect place to create a graphic organizer.*

**End of Section.**

The OSSLT Literacy Lab

17

# News Report: presents information in the form of a news story

· · · · · · · · · · · · · · · · · · · · · · · · · · · · · · · · · · · · · · · · · · · · · · · · · ·

Hello. My name is Sitarah and I am from Brampton. I often read news reports online. They answer the questions Who? What? Where? When? and How? I often had difficulties answering questions after reading a news report until my brother gave me a tip that I've used ever since. He told me to read the questions quickly before reading the report. That way, I know what to look for when reading the selection. My brother's advice usually isn't that good, and I often don't pay attention to a lot of the things he says. However, I found this tip really helpful and I now do this for all the reading activities. Try it and see if it helps you too.

**Read the selection below and answer the questions that follow it.**

# Reality prank show turns the tables on students

A high school wrestling team changed [1] its name—and mascot—from Huskies to Unicorns . This is one of the pranks played on teens from around Greater Toronto in a new, Canadian reality show which premiered Tuesday night.

The pranks were conducted at 20 schools— [2] in Brampton, Mississauga and Richmond Hill, to name a few—set up by host Lisa Gilroy with the help, and approval, of principals and teachers.

While some may question the ethics of [3] playing jokes on kids at school, the show's producer says it was deliberately harmless and all in good fun. No one teen was singled out—entire classes were involved—and everyone from principal to parent signed off on the prank before it was approved to go on air. "We basically wanted to do a prank show that had never been done before, with teachers and principals getting the kids," said Mitch Burman, supervising producer and director.

"It's a kind of double-cross; it's usually the [4] kids who are being the pranksters in class. We let the teachers and principals get a little payback."

The Peel District School Board agreed [5] to be part of the show and a Bolton high school—Humberview—was involved in transforming its wrestlers into unicorns.

Carla Pereira, manager of [6] communications for the Peel District School Board said, "The principal made it very clear that the prank needed to be pre-approved. It was reviewed by the principal and other staff, and they were also consulted on which team would be pranked."

She said the "production team was [7] very co-operative and focused on making it a positive experience for students. My understanding, from the principal, is that the students loved the experience."

The show was created by a Canadian [8] television production company. Pereira said parents were initially made aware that their children "would be videotaped for a 'commercial'—that was the prank. Students and parents signed consent afterwards to permit the footage to be aired."

Adapted from the article "Reality prank show Undercover High turns the tables on Toronto students" by Kristin Rushowy, published in *Toronto Star*, June 17, 2014. Licensed from *Toronto Star* for republication in *The OSSLT Literacy Lab*—Torstar Syndication Services.

**Reading: News Report**

**Multiple-Choice** (Circle the best or most correct answer.)

**1** Why did the wrestling team change its name from Huskies to Unicorns?

    **A** They changed schools.

    **B** They liked the new name better.

    **C** Their coach insisted they change it.

    **(D)** They were being pranked for a reality show.

**2** Why were entire classes pranked instead of individual students?

    **(A)** to prevent singling any one out

    **B** to make filming easier

    **C** to involve more people

    **D** to please the producer

**3** According to the supervising producer, what did teachers enjoy most about being part of this project?

    **A** being tricky

    **B** punishing students

    **(C)** showing students they could be fun

    **D** being on TV

**4** Which word is closest in meaning to "ethics" as used in paragraph 3?

    **A** committees

    **(B)** morals

    **C** reasons

    **D** decisions

Tip: If you don't understand a word, read the sentence before and after it, looking for clues.

**5** How is paragraph 1 organized?

    **(A)** specific details to general information

    **B** general information to specific details

    **C** chronological order

    **D** comparing and contrasting

Tip: Read the four answers and rule out any answers that are incorrect.

**Reading: News Report**

Hey there. My name is Chun and I am from Markham. To really understand a news article, I answer the five questions Who? What? Where? When? and How? I simply say the answers aloud then write them in boxes. I find this really helps me understand the article and gives me a great visual to really see what the news report was all about. It's easy to do. Try it below.

| Who? | Host Lisa Gilroy, various teachers and students in high schools were involved with the prank show. |
|---|---|

| What? | A reality TV show filmed teachers performing pranks in high schools. |
|---|---|

| Where? | It took place at twenty schools in the Greater Toronto Areas such as Brampton, Mississauga and Richmond Hill. |
|---|---|

| When? | The filming happened during the school year. The TV show premiered Tuesday night. |
|---|---|

| How? | A TV production team pranked students in various schools, filming it for a reality show. |
|---|---|

### Reading: News Report

**6** Why did students and staff find it a positive experience to be on a reality prank TV show? Use specific details from the selection to support your answer.

*Tip: Use specific and relevant details and information from the reading selection.*

The students and teachers found it to be a positive experience to be on a reality prank TV show. According to the supervision producer, the teachers enjoyed double-crossing the students. The producer states that no one teen was singled out and those filming the show focused on making it a positive experience for the students.

### Rough Notes
*Use the space below for rough notes. Nothing you write in this space will be scored.*

**End of Section.**

**Reading: News Report**

**Read the selection below and answer the questions that follow it.**

# Hitchhiking Robot to Journey Across Canada

With pool noodle arms, a plastic bucket for a torso and a limitless wealth of retrievable knowledge—at least while in the 3G network range—a curious entity is getting ready to put out the thumb and hitch rides across Canada this summer. It's HitchBOT, the genderless hitchhiking robot that will rely on the kindness of flesh-and-blood strangers to safely complete a 4,480-kilometre odyssey that starts in Halifax on July 27 and is supposed to wind up at an art gallery in Victoria. [1]

At least that's the hope. Like every cross-continental ramble, this one's a gamble. "There's this idea of adventure, exploration, optimism," said David Harris Smith, a McMaster University researcher who's spearheading the "social robotics" experiment with Ryerson's Frauke Zeller, an assistant professor in communications. [2]

"It kind of depends upon empathy and social collaboration," Harris Smith added. "That's one of the risks we're willing to take." [3]

Conceived through discussions that began last year, the HitchBOT project involves students and professors. The team is using speech-recognition software so that HitchBOT can converse with the people it meets, as well as network connectivity to allow it to search [4] for regionally-relevant talking points and post photos and text to social media.

The robot will be about the size of a six-year-old child that will include a built-in car seat that can be buckled up next to a driver. [5]

The plan is to simply leave HitchBOT on the side of the road in Halifax. When someone comes to pick it up, the robot will tell them where it's headed, and ask them how far they're going. [6]

Harris Smith said the robot's conversation software will allow it to "negotiate" the details of its ride and request to be plugged in so that it can recharge its battery. At the end of the ride, HitchBOT will ask to be left safely on the side of the road, where it will wait with its thumb out to be picked up again. [7]

Photo courtesy of HitchBOT / hitchBOT.me. Used with permission.

Adapted from the article "Hitchhiking robot to journey across Canada this summer" by Alex Ballingall, published in *Toronto Star*, June 17, 2014. Licensed from *Toronto Star* for republication in *The OSSLT Literacy Lab*—Torstar Syndication Services.

## Reading: News Report

**Multiple-Choice** (Circle the best or most correct answer.)

**1** According to the selection, what did David Harris Smith hope HitchBOT would accomplish?

 A create awareness about car seat safety

 B communicate with various people across Canada

 (C) hitchhike across Canada and rely on the kindness of strangers

 D gather information from across Canada

**2** What type of details will HitchBOT "negotiate" when it is picked up for a ride?

 (A) where it is headed and how to recharge its battery

 B regionally-relevant talking points

 C posting photos and texts to social media

 D the length of its trip

**3** What is this "social robotics" experiment really about?

 A robotic speech

 B adventure and travel

 C demonstrating the advances in robotics

 (D) empathy and co-operation

**4** Which word is closest in meaning to "odyssey" as used in paragraph 1?

 A occurrence

 B experiment

 (C) journey

 D strange

**5** Which event described in the selection happened first?

 (A) Students and professors discussed the idea of HitchBOT.

 B HitchBOT was built with pool noodle arms and a plastic bucket for a torso.

 C Speech-recognition software was installed in HitchBOT.

 D HitchBOT was dropped at the side of the road in Halifax.

Tip: Don't leave a question blank. Make an educated guess as a last resort.

**6** Why did David Harris Smith and Frauke Zeller conduct this experiment? Use specific details from the selection to support your answer.

*Tip: Reread your response and correct any errors you notice.*

David Harris Smith and Frauke Zeller conducted this experiment to see if a robot could travel across Canada based on empathy and co-operation from people. They combined robotics and social optimism and called it "social robotics." The creators realized it is a gamble, but wanted to see if HitchBOT would go from Halifax to Victoria successfully.

**Rough Notes**
*Use the space below for rough notes. Nothing you write in this space will be scored.*

**End of Section.**

# Dialogue: presents a conversation between two or more people

· · · · · · · · · · · · · · · · · · · · · · · · · · · · · · · · · · · · · · · · · · · · · · · · · ·

Hey. My name is Charlotte and I am from Barrie. Sometimes reading a dialogue will mess me up. So now, I do two things. The first thing I do is pretend that I am reading a movie script, and I visualize or play the conversation in my head as if it were a film. I even imagine details like what the people in the dialogue look like. This helps to give meaning to the conversation for me. The second thing I do is pay attention to who is talking in the dialogue. I do this by noticing "tags" or words that give me a clue that it might be a new speaker including words like "said," "paused," "exclaimed," "replied," etc. I also take note of when it is a new paragraph. This usually indicates a change in who is speaking in the dialogue.

26

**Read the selection below and answer the questions that follow it.**

Tip: The numbers at the side indicate the paragraph number.

Sofie took a deep breath and knocked on Mr. Patel's office door. 1

"Come in," called Mr. Patel. "What can I do for you?" 2

"Well," Sofie hesitated. She was nervous talking to adults. "I have an idea for fundraising for the school library." 3

"Oh," Mr. Patel raised his eyebrows. "This sounds interesting. I would like to hear what you have to say. Please share your idea, Sofie." 4

"Well, lots of people have books at home that they've read and don't need any more. What about organizing a book drive, then have a sale in the library? It would be a type of used-book fair." 5

Mr. Patel paused, "But who will sell the books and how will we get people to attend it?" 6

"I know lots of students who would love to help and my dad is good friends with a famous author. I'm sure we could get him to come in and speak." 7

"And advertising…?" 8

"We could post it on the school's website and put it in the newsletters. There is also the sign in front of the school. We could include information during morning announcements and put posters up." 9

"Sounds like you've thought this though, Sofie. I think it just might work," Mr. Patel remarked, rather impressed. 10

"Thank you, Mr. Patel." 11

Sofie thought to herself, "I didn't need to be nervous at all!" 12

Tip: Each new paragraph represents a change of speaker in this selection.

## Reading: Dialogue

**Multiple-Choice** (Circle the best or most correct answer.)

**1** Why did Sofie take a deep breath before knocking on Mr. Patel's office door?

    **A** She was tired.

    **(B)** She was nervous.

    **C** She was confident.

    **D** She did not like Mr. Patel.

**2** Why did Sofie want to talk to Mr. Patel?

    **(A)** She had a fundraising idea.

    **B** She loved books.

    **C** She wanted better grades.

    **D** She wanted to bring a famous author to the school.

**3** Which word is closest in meaning to "impressed" (paragraph 10)?

    **A** imprinted

    **B** imitated

    **C** bored

    **(D)** pleased

**4** What does "it" refer to in paragraph 6?

    **A** advertising

    **B** book drive

    **(C)** used-book fair

    **D** newsletter

*Tip: Go back and reread paragraph 6 to be sure you know what "it" is referring to.*

**5** According to the selection, what would be most persuasive to Mr. Patel about his decision to support a used-book fair?

    **A** the money that could be made

    **(B)** the details had been thought through

    **C** the advertising

    **D** the books

28

**Reading: Dialogue**

**6** Identify why you think Sofie was nervous to see Mr. Patel. Use specific details from the selection to support your answer.

Sofie was nervous to see Mr. Patel because she was

uncomfortable talking to adults. It is implied that she was

nervous because, according to the selection, she took a deep

breath before knocking on the door and she hesitated before

entering Mr. Patel's office. At the end of the selection, Sofie

realized she didn't need to be nervous.

*Tip: Go back to the reading selection to find specific and relevant details.*

**7** Identify examples of how Sofie had thoroughly thought through the details of a used-book fair. Use specific details from the selection to support your answer.

Sofie had thoroughly thought through the details of the used-book fair as

she had thoughtful and organized answers to all of Mr. Patel's questions.

For example, she had a method of gathering the books and her father

knew an author who could come to the school and speak. In addition,

Sofie had a solid advertising plan of using the school website, newsletters,

announcements, signage and posters to spread the word about the sale.

**Rough Notes**
*Use the space below for rough notes. Nothing you write in this space will be scored.*

**End of Section.**

The OSSLT Literacy Lab     29

### Reading: Dialogue

**Read the selection below and answer the questions that follow it.**

Connor packed his suitcase and sighed as he squeezed it shut. He didn't particularly want to work at a camp as a counselor-in-training this summer, but his parents had insisted he do something "productive" with his time off.    1

"Are you ready to go?" Connor's dad called up the stairs.    2

"Almost," Connor quipped back. He picked up his suitcase in one hand and grabbed his phone in the other. He just received a text and was curious who it might be.    3

"I'm coming," Connor said as he made his way down the stairs.    4

"Great. Let's put that suitcase in the car and get going before heavy traffic sets in."    5

Connor started to read his text. It was from his good friend, Raj.    6

"Who's that from?" Connor's dad queried as he started the car engine.    7

"Raj."    8

"Oh, that's nice. He's probably wishing you luck as a counselor-in-training."    9

"You know, Connor, I completely understand that you aren't too excited about leaving your friends and going up north. But this will be such a terrific experience. You will meet new people, take on responsibility and get volunteer hours too. The lake at the camp is fabulous. I really think you are going to warm to the idea as time goes on."    10

"Yes, I think you are right, Dad," Connor answered.    11

Connor's dad was surprised by the change in tone in his son's voice. "Well, you sound a lot more chipper," he exclaimed.    12

"I am," Connor smiled mischievously. "You know that was Raj who texted me, right?"    13

"Yes."    14

Connor was laughing, "His parents have signed him up to be a counselor-in-training at the same camp."    15

His father smiled, "Well, what do you know? That's good news for Raj, you and me."    16

**30**

**Multiple-Choice** (Circle the best or most correct answer.)

**1** What is the purpose of this reading selection?

    **A** to compare summer camps

    **B** to describe driving

    **(C)** to entertain with an anecdote

    **D** to explain counselor-in-training

**2** What had Connor's parents insisted he do this summer?

    **A** get a job

    **B** go to camp

    **C** spend time with Raj

    **(D)** be productive

**3** Which is closest in meaning to "queried" as used in paragraph 7?

    **(A)** asked

    **B** answered

    **C** yelled

    **D** said

*Tip: Go back and reread the sentence in the selection replacing "queried" with each option.*

**4** Which of the following is **not** a reason Connor's father listed for working as a counselor-in-training?

    **A** to meet new people

    **(B)** to get away from friends

    **C** to take on responsibility

    **D** to get volunteer hours

**5** Why did Connor sound a lot happier after getting the text from Raj?

    **A** Connor no longer had to go to camp.

    **B** Raj was going to visit Connor.

    **(C)** Raj was going to be a counselor-in-training at the same camp.

    **D** Raj was coming over to say good-bye.

**Turn the page to complete this section.**

### Reading: Dialogue

**6** Why did Connor's father want Connor to be a counselor-in-training? Use specific details from the selection to support your answer.

Connor's father wanted Connor to be a counselor-in-training so that he would be doing something worthwhile and productive in the summer. Connor's father felt there were multiple benefits to being a counselor-in-training to Connor. This is seen in the selection when Connor's father says to Connor, "You will meet new people, take on responsibility and get volunteer hours too."

**7** Why was Raj's text good news for Raj, Connor and Connor's father? Use specific details from the selection to support your answer.

Connor's father was happy about Raj's news because his son was more enthusiastic about the summer experience of being a counselor-in-training. Raj was happy because he would be able to be with his friend during the summer. Connor was happy because, even though he had to do something "productive" as indicated in paragraph 1, he would have his friend there to share the experience with.

**Rough Notes**
*Use the space below for rough notes. Nothing you write in this space will be scored.*

**End of Section.**

# **Real-Life Narrative:** presents an account of a significant time in an individual's life

· · · · · · · · · · · · · · · · · · · · · · · · · · · · · · · · · · · · · · · · · · · · · · ·

Hello there. My name is Aiden and I am from Toronto. I really enjoy reading real-life narratives—especially if they are about a person I am interested in. To make sure I understand a narrative, I scan the first and last paragraphs to get an idea of what it is about. Then, when I read the entire narrative I try to look for links between what I am reading and the experiences I have had in my own life. I find when I connect what I am reading to things I already know, I enjoy it more and understand it better.

**Reading: Real-Life Narrative**

**Read the selection below and answer the questions that follow it.**

# Adam Beach is a Role Model

Photo courtesy of the Canadian Film Centre/Phillip Chin

After a long list of over 60 film and TV roles, actor Adam Beach was excited to return to Canada to star in the TV series *Arctic Air*, which ran from 2012–2014. Adam played the character of Bobby Martin. This starring role gave Adam mainstream notoriety here at home in Canada. [1]

Adam, a member of the Ojibwa Nation, has worked alongside many actors in both Canada and in the U.S. including the likes of Harrison Ford and Daniel Craig. [2]

Adam was born in Ashern, Manitoba, and when he was young, he and his two brothers lived on the Lake Manitoba Dog Creek First Nation Reserve. Adam's rise to fame wasn't without challenges, however—when Adam was only eight years old, his parents died only months apart. Adam and his brother went to live with his grandmother until he was 12. Then the boys were taken to Winnipeg where they stayed with an aunt and uncle. [3]

While in high school, Adam discovered drama. He began performing in local theatre productions and took a lead role at the Manitoba Theatre for Young People. [4]

In recent years, Adam has started several charity initiatives and believes in giving back to his community. There is a special spot in his heart for youth and film, and he supports both. He is involved with the National Aboriginal Achievement Foundation. He also travels to schools, conferences and other events to speak candidly about the challenges he has faced in his life and his road to success. [5]

Of his role on *Arctic Air*, Adam talks about his connection to Bobby, the character he plays: "I do a lot of inspirational talks for kids, to motivate them to change their lives and give them hope. And I found that this character shares a lot of those qualities. A lot of the communities I connect to get their inspiration from television and YouTube. I felt that this character could reach out to them and really connect. He's a character who's struggling with himself. He's trying to get back in touch with the person he once was."

6

Beyond playing roles on TV, Adam has proved he is also a role model, spreading hope and also encouragement. Although acting in *Arctic Air* has been a major part of his career, who knows what's next for Adam Beach?

7

Tip: If you read a word you don't understand, look for a root word you may know inside a larger word.

© Feature flash I Dreamstime.com - Adam Beach Photo

## Reading: Real-Life Narrative

**Multiple-Choice** (Circle the best or most correct answer.)

**1** Which of the following is Adam Beach's birthplace?

   **A** Winnipeg

   **B** Ojibwa

   **(C)** Ashbern

   **D** Dog Creek

**2** At what point did Adam first become interested in acting?

   **(A)** when he was in high school

   **B** when he went to live with his grandmother

   **C** when he was chosen to act in *Arctic Air*

   **D** when he acted with Harrison Ford and Daniel Craig

**3** Which word is closest in meaning to "notoriety" as used in paragraph 1?

   **A** disrepute

   **(B)** fame

   **C** influence

   **D** publicity

**4** What are two focuses of Adam's charities?

   **A** television and film

   **B** high school and community

   **C** drama and film

   **(D)** youth and film

**5** Why are commas used in paragraph 2?

   **A** They link two independent clauses.

   **B** They separate items in a series.

   **(C)** They set off added information.

   **D** They set off introductory elements.

**6** What best describes paragraph 6?

   **(A)** a direct quote

   **B** an indirect quote

   **C** an illustration

   **D** a description

**7** According to the selection, what is the most likely reason Adam feels the need to share his story as an inspirational speaker?

   **A** to gain notoriety

   **B** to promote and encourage people to watch television

   **(C)** to encourage children who are facing challenges

   **D** to promote *Arctic Air*

**8** Why is paragraph 7 an effective conclusion?

   **A** It provides unusual information about Adam.

   **(B)** The question suggests that Adam has future accomplishments.

   **C** It adds additional information.

   **D** It introduces a new idea.

Tip: If necessary, reread relevant parts of the narrative to choose the best answer.

**End of Section.**

**Read the selection below and answer the questions that follow it.**

# Eileen Vollick

Photo Credit: Canada Aviation and Space Museum

On March 13, 1928, 19-year-old Eileen Vollick took the day off work in order to take her federal aviation test. The textile analyst, who worked for the Hamilton Cotton Company, successfully passed the flight test to become the first woman in Canada to qualify as a pilot as well as the first woman in the world to be trained on a ski plane.

Although this event granted Eileen a sort of "celebrity-status," it was not always an easy path for this Wiarton-born textile analyst and assistant designer. Eileen had watched pilots take off and land at Jack V. Elliott's Air Service and wanted the opportunity to fly herself.

Eileen applied for flight training, but because she was a woman, Jack Elliot wouldn't accept her as a student until the Department of National Defense gave their approval. The Department took three months to approve her application and insisted she be 19 years old even though the age requirement for men was 17. While waiting to turn 19, Eileen became the first Canadian woman to parachute out on the wings of a Curtiss JN-4 plane and parachuted into Hamilton Bay, which is now known as Burlington Bay.

The first flight instructor assigned to her didn't want a female student so—even though it was against the rules—he did spins, loops, and zooms on the first lesson. He was attempting to frighten Eileen, but it didn't work.

However, Eileen's next two instructors welcomed her. She also felt accepted by her 35 classmates who were all male students. Eileen had to take her lessons at 6 a.m.

**Reading: Real-Life Narrative**

throughout the winter so she could get to work by 8:30 a.m. Determination and hard work were small sacrifices to reach her goal.

It took courage and determination for women to be fully accepted in the new flying movement. Some women weren't allowed to sign up for lessons, and others were subjected to a more rigorous set of rules or they faced instructors who tried to scare them off. However, women in aviation grew in numbers and impact thanks in no small part to Eileen Vollick for bravely becoming Canada's first female pilot.

6

Photo Credit: Canada Aviation and Space Museum

Tip: If a long sentence is confusing, reread it and put it in your own words.

**Reading: Real-Life Narrative**

**Multiple-Choice** (Circle the best or most correct answer.)

**1** Why did Eileen want to become a pilot?

**(A)** She had watched pilots take off and land at an airport.

**B** She wanted to become the first female pilot in Canada.

**C** She wanted to help Canada's efforts in the war.

**D** She enjoyed taking on a challenge.

**2** What was **not** one of Eileen's accomplishments?

**A** first woman to be trained on a ski plane

**(B)** first woman to fly solo

**C** first woman to parachute from a Curtiss JN-4 plane

**D** first Canadian woman to qualify as a pilot

**3** Which word is closest in meaning to "rigorous" as used in paragraph 6?

**A** careful

**B** accurate

**C** attentive

**(D)** demanding

**4** What was one thing that Eileen did that demonstrated her determination?

**A** She quit her regular job as a textile analyst.

**B** She listened to critical comments from male students.

**(C)** She took her lessons early in the morning before she went to work.

**D** She broke rules while flying.

**5** Why are two dashes used in paragraph 4?

**(A)** to emphasize the content between the dashes

**B** to clarify a list in the sentence

**C** to add descriptiveness to the sentence

**D** to join words in the sentence

**6** Why did Jack Elliot finally allow Eileen to take flight training?

**(A)** She received approval from The Department of Defence.

**B** She turned 17 years old.

**C** She had already parachuted from a Curtiss JN-4.

**D** She had already performed spins, loops and zooms.

**7** What is the purpose of paragraphs 3, 4 and 5?

**A** to show the ways different people supported Eileen

**B** to describe the typical life of a pilot

**(C)** to describe the challenges Eileen faced

**D** to add humour to the story

**End of Section.**

**Graphic Text:** presents ideas and information with the help of graphic features, such as diagrams, photographs, drawings, sketches, patterns, timetables, maps, charts or tables

. . . . . . . . . . . . . . . . . . . . . . . . . . . . . . . . . . . . . . . . . . . . . . . . . . . . . . . .

Hi. I'm Jia and I am from Harrow. When I look at graphic text, I always read the title and headings first to see what the selection is all about. Then I pay attention to the "picture" part of the material. Finally, I read all the text, paying attention to what the text says about the graphics.

40

**Reading: Graphic Text**

**Read the selection below and answer the questions that follow it.**

# Life Cycle of a Frog

*Tip: Read the title first and look at the illustrations before reading the details.*

**1** Female frogs lay eggs in water in a string or mass that adheres to vegetation. Then the male frog fertilizes the eggs while they are being laid. The outside layer of a fertilized egg is jelly-like and swells in the water to form a protective coating.

**2** Within 2 to 25 days the egg hatches into a tadpole. A tadpole swims more like a fish than a frog.

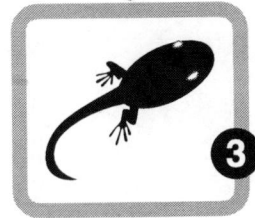

**3** As the tadpole develops and grows, it forms gills that allow it to breathe more efficiently underwater. As it continues to grow longer, a fin forms to allow the tadpole to swim better. The tadpole starts to grow hind legs.

**4** Next, the tadpole's front legs develop. The tail becomes shorter and the tadpole's gills are replaced with lungs.

**5** The young frog grows and matures to adulthood. The adult frogs then lay their eggs and begin the cycle again.

The OSSLT Literacy Lab

41

### Reading: Graphic Text

**Multiple-Choice** (Circle the best or most correct answer.)

**1** According to the selection, where do frogs most often lay their eggs?

    **A** on the shore

    **B** in the trees

    **(C)** in the water

    **D** in the sand

**2** Which word is closest in meaning to "develops" as used in Stage 3?

    **A** declines

    **B** slows

    **(C)** matures

    **D** diminishes

**3** Which feature in this graphic text best identifies chronological order?

    **A** title

    **(B)** numbers

    **C** pictures

    **D** text

**4** Which stage could be considered both the beginning and the end of the life cycle of a frog?

    **A** Stage 1

    **B** Stage 2

    **C** Stage 4

    **(D)** Stage 5

**5** When does a tadpole become a better swimmer?

    **(A)** when it forms a fin

    **B** when it forms gills

    **C** when it forms front legs

    **D** when it forms hind legs

*Tip: Rephrase question 5 as a statement using each answer in the sentence to see which is correct.*

**End of Section.**

**Reading: Graphic Text**

**Read the selection below and answer the questions that follow it.**

# South City Community Pool Schedule

Hours of operation: weekdays: 10:00 a.m.–6:00 p.m.     weekends: 10:00 a.m.–4:00 p.m.

| Time | Mon | Tues | Wed | Thus | Fri | Sat | Sun |
|---|---|---|---|---|---|---|---|
| 10:00 a.m. | adult laps | aqua fit | laps | aqua fit | adult laps | laps | aqua fit |
| 11:00 a.m. | parent & tots | school groups | parents & tots | school groups | aqua fit | family swim | lessons |
| 12:00 noon | aqua fit | parent & tots | school groups | parents & tots | school groups | family swim | family swim |
| 1:00 p.m. | lessons | aqua fit | lessons | lessons | school groups | lessons | family swim |
| 2:00 p.m. | diving club | swim team practice | diving club | school groups | diving club | lessons | family swim |
| 3 p.m. | free swim | lessons | free swim | lessons | free swim | lessons | family swim |
| 4 p.m. | lessons | laps | laps | free swim | lessons | closed | closed |
| 5 p.m. | laps | free swim | lessons | laps | swim team practice | closed | closed |

**Descriptions:**

**Adult laps:** The pool is divided into lanes and is open for lap swimming for adults over the age of 18.

**\*Aqua fit**: Aqua fit offers exercise classes in the pool. Check front desk for more information and registration. There is an extra fee for aqua fit.

**Diving club:** The South City Community Diving Club uses the pool at this time.

**Family swim:** This is a time for parents and children to enjoy the pool. The slide is open at this time.

**Free swim:** Open for all to come and enjoy the pool. The slide is open at this time.

**Laps:** The pool is divided into lanes and is open for swimming.

**\*Lessons:** The South City Community Pool offers lessons to swimmers of all ages and skill levels. Check with the front desk for more information and registration. There is an extra fee for lessons.

**Parents & tots:** The pool is open for parents and their children under the age of four. All children must be accompanied by an adult.

**School groups:** This time is available to various local schools to book in advance.

**Swim team practice.** The South City Community Swim Team has designated practice time.

*\*Registration is required for these activities. An additional fee will apply.*

The OSSLT Literacy Lab

**43**

### Reading: Graphic Text

**Multiple-Choice** (Circle the best or most correct answer.)

**1** Which activities require registration and an extra fee?

   **A** parents & tots

   **B** free swim and laps

   **C** school groups and adult laps

   **(D)** aqua fit and lessons

**2** How is the schedule organized?

   **A** by comparing and contrasting

   **(B)** by chronological order

   **C** by cause and effect

   **D** in order of importance

**3** According to the schedule, when can a 12-year-old child go to the pool to swim laps?

   **A** Monday, 10:00 a.m.

   **(B)** Tuesday, 4:00 p.m.

   **C** Friday, 11:00 p.m.

   **D** Saturday, 2:00 p.m.

**4** Which feature of this graphic text identifies the schedule?

   **A** arrows

   **B** description

   **(C)** table

   **D** lessons

**5** According to the schedule, if you wanted to use the recreational slide, when would be the best time to go to South City Community Pool?

   **(A)** Sunday, 12 noon

   **B** Tuesday, 4 p.m.

   **C** Monday, 12 noon

   **D** Wednesday, 5 p.m.

**6** What is the purpose of the asterisks (*) beside "aqua fit" and "lessons" in the description?

   **(A)** to direct the reader to additional information about those activities

   **B** to highlight those activities

   **C** to help readers understand the schedule better

   **D** to improve the appearance of the schedule.

Tip: Go back to the selection to find all the places where asterisks (*) occur.

**End of Section.**

44

# SECTION 2

# Section 2: The OSSLT Writing Lab

The OSSLT assesses your skills through a variety of writing tasks.

- **Long-writing tasks:** There are two kinds of long-writing tasks: a news report and a series of paragraphs expressing an opinion.
    1. **News report:** You will be required to write a news report based on the picture and headline provided.
    2. **A series of paragraphs expressing an opinion:** You will be required to write a minimum of three paragraphs, which include an introduction, development and conclusion. You will be given two lined pages for your written work.
- **Short-writing tasks:** These tasks will give you the opportunity to demonstrate your writing skills using your knowledge and personal experience. Responses must be written in complete sentences. Students are given six lines for their response.
- **Multiple-choice tasks:** These tasks will give you the opportunity to demonstrate the three writing skills of developing a main idea, organizing information and using conventions.

For the OSSLT, "writing" is defined as communicating in the forms in which students are expected to write. Through a combination of short- and long-writing tasks, the OSSLT focuses on three writing skills:

1. developing a main idea with sufficient supporting details;
2. organizing information and ideas in a coherent manner; and
3. using conventions (syntax, spelling, grammar, punctuation) in a manner that does not distract from clear communication.

The lined space provided for written work indicates the approximate length of the writing expected. **Be sure to respond in complete sentences.**

In this resource, you will be walked through two examples of each type of writing activity similar to those you will encounter on the OSSLT. You will find advice from fictional representations of typical Ontario students. Tips will be provided in the form of notes that are "paper-clipped" to your activities for ease of reference.

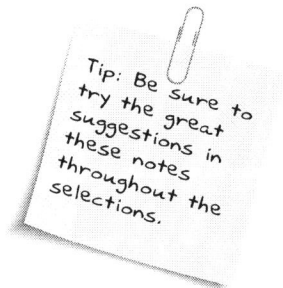

*Tip: Be sure to try the great suggestions in these notes throughout the selections.*

You will know you have completed a section when you see the phrase "End of Section." in a grey rectangular box.

**End of Section.**

---

Information found on EQAO website. Check frequently for accuracy and updates.

# News Report: presents information in the form of a news story

Hey. What's happening? My name is Liam and I live in Sharbot Lake. Writing news reports is a bit of a process for me because it isn't something I have to do very often in my day-to-day life. What I find challenging is making up all the details. It requires a bit of imagination. Other than the headline and the picture, there isn't anywhere to find actual details. So, this process requires me to make things up. I map out my Who? What? Where? When? Why? and How? first. Then I go on to list the participants who will be in my story and I write out two direct quotes and one indirect quote before even starting to write the actual article. After organizing my content in a logical way, I write the report in third person. Unless it is a direct quote I use words like "he," "she," "you," instead of words like "me," "I," "us," or "we." Once I got the hang of it, writing news reports can be fun and creative.

The OSSLT Literacy Lab

47

Writing: News Report

### Writing a News Report

| | |
|---|---|
| **Task:** | Write a **news report** on page 51 based on the headline and picture below.<br>• You will have to make up the facts and information to answer some or all of the following questions: Who? What? Where? When? Why? How?<br>• You must relate your newspaper report to **both** the headline **and** the picture. |
| **Purpose and Audience:** | to report on an event for the readers of a newspaper |
| **Length:** | The lined space provided for your written work indicates the approximate length of the writing expected. |

## Students Raise Money for Local Charity

**Rough Notes**
*Use the space below for rough notes. Nothing you write in this space will be scored.*

*Tip: Look carefully at the headline AND the photo.*

*Write your report on the lines provided on page 51.*

**Writing: News Report**

Hi there. My name is Abigail and I am from Kitchener. I always get organized before writing a news report. After I carefully read the headline and look at the photo, I fill out a Who? What? Where? When? Why? and How? organizer. Fill out the one below to get you started.

Who? (List all the participants who will be in your article. This information comes from the title, the picture and **your imagination.**)

students of Everywhere H.S., Brook Thomas, Cooper Phillips and

Tiffany Ripley

What?

charity car wash

Where?

school parking lot

When?

weekend of June 15

Why?

to raise money for the

local food bank

How?

Students organized a car wash, advertised it and volunteered their

time to raise $3,500 for the local food bank.

The OSSLT Literacy Lab

49

The OSSLT Literacy Lab Answer Key and Teacher's Guide                    55

**Writing: News Report**

Hello. I'm Dhilan and I live in Oshawa. Something that really helped me write a great news report was understanding and using direct and indirect quotes. If you read the newspaper, most articles have them. Direct quotes are the exact words someone says and they are surrounded by quotation marks. Here is an example: "The students were great. They organized the car wash with very little input from the staff," Principal Barker explained. Indirect quotes take the information someone said, but do not share them word-for-word. Here is an example: Educators say that hundreds of students organized a charity car wash completely on their own. Using both types of quotes adds flavour and details to your report.

Using your imagination, create two direct quotes and one indirect quote you can incorporate into your news report based on the headline "Students Raise Money for Charity" and the photo on page 48.

"We wanted to do something that would benefit the community," Student Association President, Brook Thomas said.

"We gave up time on the weekend, but it was fun and our efforts went to a good cause," Cooper Phillips commented.

Tip: Make sure your direct quotes are inside quotation marks.

Students certainly can make a difference, at least that is what teachers at Everywhere High School say.

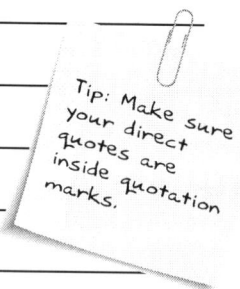

# Students Raise Money for Local Charity

 Students certainly can make a difference; at least that is what teachers at Everywhere High say.

 The Grade 10 students of Everywhere High School organized a car wash that was held on June 15 in the school parking lot. All proceeds were donated to the local food bank.

 "We wanted to do something that would benefit the community," Student Association President, Brooke Thomas said.

 Students came together a few weeks ago to organize, advertise and volunteer at the car wash after learning that supplies at the local food bank were at an all-time low.

 The idea was the brainchild of Tiffany Ripley, who was obtaining volunteer hours at the food bank. She brought the idea to Brooke Thomas and a committee was formed to organize the event.

 Even though they were volunteers, students appeared to enjoy themselves. Cooper Phillips, a Grade 10 student commented, "We gave up time on the weekend, but it was fun and our efforts went to a good cause."

*Tip: Read your report when you are finished writing to see if it makes sense.*

 The car wash was well-supported by the community and the students raised over $3,500 for the food bank.

*Tip: Organize your report in a logical manner using the information from your graphic organizers.*

**End of Section.**

### Writing: News Report

### Writing a News Report

| | |
|---|---|
| **Task:** | Write a **news report** on the following page based on the headline and picture below. |
| | • You will have to make up the facts and information to answer some or all of the following questions: Who? What? Where? When? Why? How? |
| | • You must relate your newspaper report to **both** the headline **and** the picture. |
| **Purpose and Audience:** | to report on an event for the readers of a newspaper |
| **Length:** | The lined space provided for your written work indicates the approximate length of the writing expected. |

## Students Demand Healthy Choices in School Cafeteria

**Rough Notes**
*Use the space below for rough notes. Nothing you write in this space will be scored.*

*Tip: If you don't have enough space here, use scrap paper to organize your thoughts.*

*Write your report on the lines provided on the following page.*

# Students Demand Healthy Choices in School Cafeteria

Shane Doran was not impressed with the food choices at Nowhere High School. In the running for the Canadian Rugby Team, Doran wanted to make sure he was in top physical form. And, wise food choices was part of his routine.

"I wanted to see more vegetables, salads and healthy options. I like pizza and fries as much as the next guy, but I know that it is important for me to have a more well-balanced diet for me to perform optimally. I just had to do something to change things."

Doran and some of his friends started a petition, gaining over 800 signatures asking for more fresh fruit and vegetable options in the cafeteria.

Principal Joanne Whyte was open to the petition and actually very impressed with how Doran and his committee handled the situation. "It is great to see students taking initiatives to change things for the better."

Whyte took the petition to the local school board and changes were implemented within two months.

Now the cafeteria features a salad bar and offers more fresh fruits and vegetables. Most students are happy about the new offerings that give students and staff more selection.

Tip: Double-check to make sure you wrote the report in third person.

**End of Section.**

# Long-Writing Tasks: presents an introduction, development and conclusion in the form of an opinion

Hi. I'm Kaitlyn and I am from Thornbury. Expressing my opinion in a series of paragraphs takes some planning for me. First, I decide what my opinion on the assigned topic is and then write that down. I then add supporting details. Finally, I put it all together, making sure that it is logical and has at least three paragraphs. I've heard from my teacher, though, that students who write more than the minimum three paragraphs tend to average higher scores on the long-writing questions.

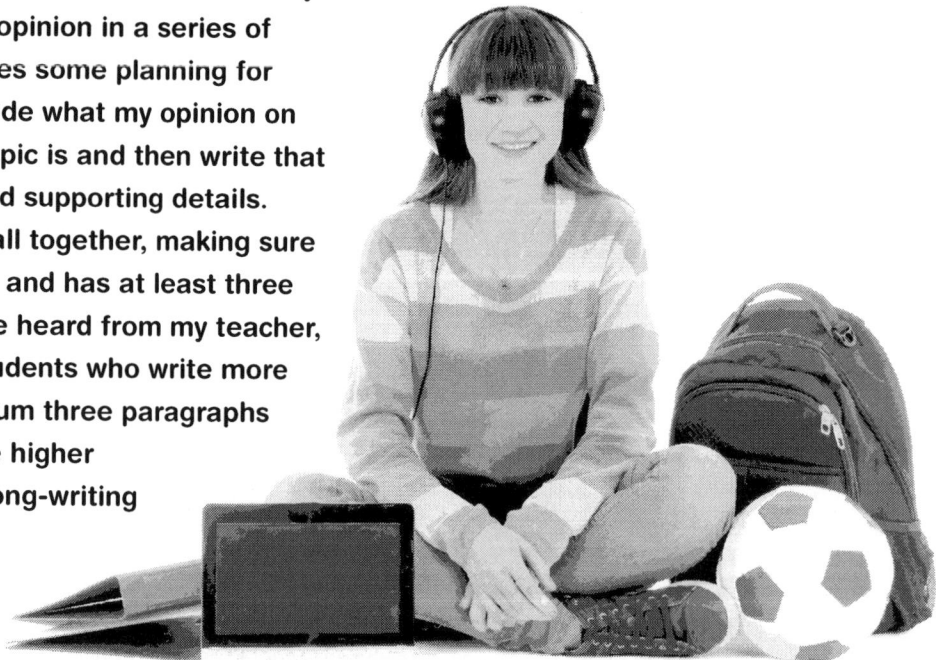

54

**Writing: Long-Writing Tasks**

## Writing a Series of Paragraphs

| | |
|---|---|
| **Task:** | Write a **minimum** of **three paragraphs** expressing an **opinion** on the topic below. Develop your main idea with supporting details (proof, facts, examples, etc.) |
| **Purpose and Audience:** | an adult who is interested in your opinion |
| **Length:** | The lined space provided for your written work indicates the approximate length of the writing expected. |
| **Topic:** | Should it be mandatory that students stay in school until they are 18 years old? |

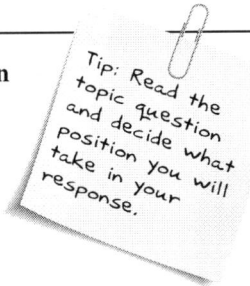

*Tip: Read the topic question and decide what position you will take in your response.*

*Write your series of paragraphs on the lines provided on pages 57-58.*

**Rough Notes**
*Use the space below for rough notes. Nothing you write in this space will be scored.*

**Writing: Long-Writing Tasks**

Should it be mandatory that students stay in school until they are 18 years old?

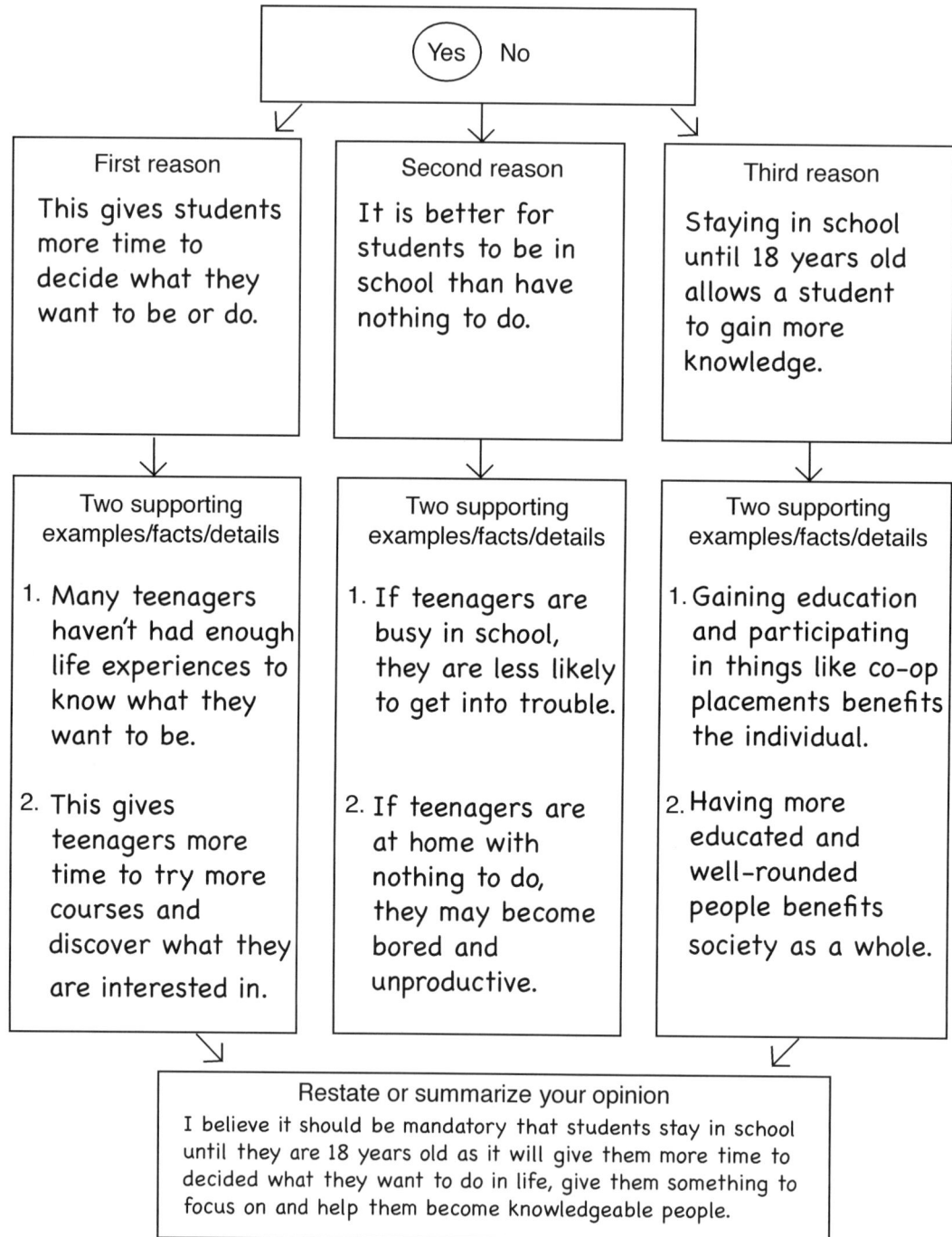

| (Yes) No |
| --- |

| First reason | Second reason | Third reason |
| --- | --- | --- |
| This gives students more time to decide what they want to be or do. | It is better for students to be in school than have nothing to do. | Staying in school until 18 years old allows a student to gain more knowledge. |

| Two supporting examples/facts/details | Two supporting examples/facts/details | Two supporting examples/facts/details |
| --- | --- | --- |
| 1. Many teenagers haven't had enough life experiences to know what they want to be.<br><br>2. This gives teenagers more time to try more courses and discover what they are interested in. | 1. If teenagers are busy in school, they are less likely to get into trouble.<br><br>2. If teenagers are at home with nothing to do, they may become bored and unproductive. | 1. Gaining education and participating in things like co-op placements benefits the individual.<br><br>2. Having more educated and well-rounded people benefits society as a whole. |

Restate or summarize your opinion

I believe it should be mandatory that students stay in school until they are 18 years old as it will give them more time to decided what they want to do in life, give them something to focus on and help them become knowledgeable people.

**Should it be mandatory that students stay in school until they are 18 years old?**

I believe that it should be mandatory that students stay in school until they are 18 years old. This will allow students to reach their full-potential before making some important life decisions.

Firstly, staying in school until you are at least 18 years old, gives students time to decided what they would like to do for a career. Often times, students come back to high school for an extra year after graduation just to get more courses and experience. Many teenagers haven't had enough life experiences to know what they want to do next in their lives. They need more time to discover what things they are interested in before making decisions about career or continuing education.

Secondly, I believe that it is better for students to be in school than to have nothing to do. If students are not busy, they are more likely to get into trouble. If teenagers are at home and have nothing to do, they can become bored and unproductive. This feeling of "lack of purpose" isn't helpful to anyone.

Tip: clearly state your opinion at the beginning and end of your response.

*Continue writing your series of paragraphs on the next page.*

**Writing: Long-Writing Tasks**

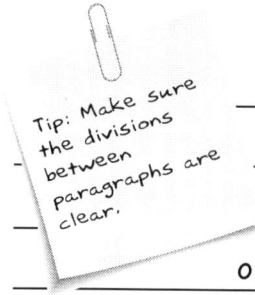

*Tip: Make sure the divisions between paragraphs are clear.*

Thirdly, staying in school until a student is 18 years old allows students more opportunity to learn more.  Gaining education better prepares students for their future. And, sometimes students take more of an interest in things the older they get. Being in school makes people better themselves. In addition, educated individuals make for a better society.

In summary, I believe it should be mandatory that students stay in school until they are 18 years old. Doing so will give students more time to decide what they want to do next in life; whether it be work or more schooling. It will also allow students to have something to focus on. And, making it mandatory for students to stay in school until they are 18 years old allows them to become knowledgeable individuals, which also makes society as a whole more knowledgeable.

**End of Section.**

## Writing a Series of Paragraphs

| | |
|---|---|
| **Task:** | Write a **minimum** of **three paragraphs** expressing an **opinion** on the topic below. Develop your main idea with supporting details (proof, facts, examples, etc.) |
| **Purpose and Audience:** | an adult who is interested in your opinion |
| **Length:** | The lined space provided for your written work indicates the approximate length of the writing expected. |
| **Topic:** | Should the government spend money on space exploration? |

*Write your series of paragraphs on the lines provided on the following two pages.*

### Rough Notes

*Use the space below for rough notes. Nothing you write in this space will be scored.*

Tip: Use this section to make a graphic organizer.

**Writing: Long-Writing Tasks**

**Should the government spend money on space exploration?**

*Tip: Write at least three paragraphs. Include an introduction, development and a conclusion.*

I believe that the government should not spend money on space exploration. Although space exploration has many benefits, I believe that it should be funded by individuals and private companies. The government gets a lot of its revenue from taxes and I believe that tax money should be spent on other issues that affect people on a more local level.

Firstly, I believe that we have a lot of issues right here at home that could benefit from funding that are more important than space exploration. A lot of people here find it hard to make enough money to get by and the use of food banks is on the rise. I feel that the government should spend more money on helping subsidize food and housing.

Secondly, I think that going to college and university is very expensive. I feel that more help from the government for students wanting an education would help a lot of individuals. That way, going to school wouldn't be such a burden to families.

Thirdly, I think that making sure that the health care system is good is more important than space exploration. Some medications and

*Continue writing your series of paragraphs on the next page.*

60

**Writing: Long-Writing Tasks**

procedures are currently not covered by OHIP and it is difficult for some families with health issues to cope. I think that this would benefit taxpayers more than space exploration.

For example, my grandmother became sick last year and had to get chemotherapy. Although that was covered by OHIP, she became very sick to her stomach. The only drug that would help her deal with her upset stomach was not covered by OHIP and cost a lot of money. If the government would use more tax money for those types of things instead of space exploration, it would make life for many families a little bit easier.

*Tip: Support your opinion with reasons and relevant examples or facts.*

Even though many experiments were performed in space, new and innovative ways for purifying water were created and other achievements have helped improve life here on earth, I believe that space exploration shouldn't be funded by the government. This type of advancement and exploration should be funded by interested individuals and organizations. I believe that the government—who uses our taxes—should fund things that are local and important to its citizens here on earth.

**End of Section.**

# Short-Writing Tasks: demonstrate the three writing skills of developing a main idea, organizing information and using conventions.

· · · · · · · · · · · · · · · · · · · · · · · · · · · · · · · · · · · · · · · · · · · · · · · · · · · · · · · ·

I'm Ben and I live in Sioux Lookout. Personally, I actually like short-writing tasks. I think what I like most about them is that I am able to use my own knowledge and experience in the answer instead of having to rely on what other people have said. I develop one main idea and I like finding specific examples, details and relevant information to support my answer.

62

**Writing: Short-Writing Tasks**

**Short-Writing Task** (Answer in full and correctly written sentences.)

**1** Should teenagers have part-time jobs? Use specific details to explain why or why not.

I believe that teenagers should not have part-time jobs. In my opinion, part-time jobs take time away from studying and extracurricular activities. Teenagers need to focus on their studies and interests while in school. Most people spend the rest of their lives working, so I feel that teenagers need to enjoy their youth before entering the work force.

*Tip: Be sure to use complete sentences.*

**Rough Notes**
*Use the space below for rough notes. Nothing you write in this space will be scored.*

*Tip: It is a good idea to read and reread the question carefully.*

**End of Section.**

**Writing: Short-Writing Tasks**

**Short-Writing Task** (Answer in full and correctly written sentences.)

**1** Should every teenager play sports? Use specific details to explain why or why not.

*Tip: Reread your response and correct any errors.*

I believe that every teenager should play sports. Sports allow teens to stay active and fit. In addition, team sports also offer a chance for teens to feel part of a group, and give them a sense of belonging and purpose. Finally, sports give teenagers something to do in their spare time; consequently, keeping them from other activities that may not be as positive.

**Rough Notes**
*Use the space below for rough notes. Nothing you write in this space will be scored.*

**End of Section.**

# Multiple-Choice Questions:
demonstrate use of writing conventions such as syntax, spelling, grammar and punctuation

· · · · · · · · · · · · · · · · · · · · · · · · · · · · · · · · · · · · · · · · · · ·

Hello. My name is Davina. I am from London. If I am not careful, the multiple-choice questions can confuse me. I have developed a couple of strategies that really help, though. First, I read and reread the question carefully. Then I read the four answers and rule out any that are incorrect. Sometimes two of them both seem right so I try to choose the *best* or *most* correct answer. I never leave a multiple-choice question blank even if I am not sure of the answer.

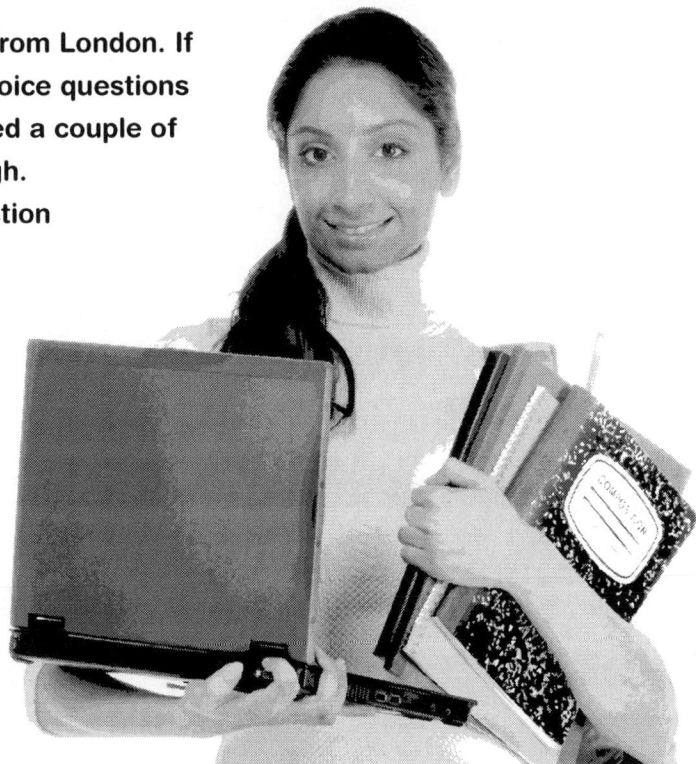

## Writing: Multiple-Choice

**Multiple-Choice** (Circle the best or most correct answer.)

**1**    Choose the sentence that is written correctly.

    (**A**) Olivia asked, "How are you?"

    **B**   Ethan answered, "I am fine".

    **C**   Emma stated "It is cold outside."

    **D**   Lucas queried, 'what day is the dance?'

*Tip: Look at the punctuation carefully in question #1.*

**2**    How is the following paragraph organized?

**There are many differences between apples and oranges. Although they are both fruit, oranges have a much thicker skin and need to be peeled in order to eat easily. On the other hand, apples can be eaten skin and all. They are both popular fruit and many people enjoy these healthy and tasty foods.**

    **A**   by order of importance

    **B**   by cause and effect

    **C**   by chronological order

    (**D**) by comparison and contrast

**3**    Choose the sentence that is written correctly.

    **A**   Jade is going too the park.

    **B**   Logan wants to go to.

    (**C**) Madison loves pandas too.

    **D**   Owen wants too see his friend.

**4**    Choose the sentence that is written correctly

    **A**   Maya attended central Secondary school.

    **B**   Mr. Maltby taught a Class in Phys. Ed.

    **C**   East Secondary School had a great Selection of Computer classes.

    (**D**) Jackson went to school in Orangeville.

66

     

**Multiple-Choice** (Circle the best or most correct answer.)

**1** Choose the sentence that is written correctly.

    **A** Me and Riley are going to the mall.

    **B** My mom gave snacks to Ava and I.

    **C** Ryan and me went swimming.

    **(D)** Hannah and I went to a concert.

**2** Which sentence does not belong in the paragraph?

(1) **Volunteering benefits young people. (2) It gives them skills and teaches them responsibility. (3) Volunteering helps them gain valuable experience for future decisions. (4) Many retired people volunteer. (5) Volunteering is a great way to prepare for the future.**

    **A** Sentence 2

    **B** Sentence 3

    **(C)** Sentence 4

    **D** Sentence 5

**3** Choose the sentence that is written correctly.

    **(A)** Nicholas is turning 16 next week.

    **B** Peyton want to know how old you are.

    **C** Isabella and Jacob is hungry.

    **D** Matt were going to see him.

**4** Choose the sentence that is written correctly

    **A** The vacation photo's were on the computer.

    **B** Our houses door was broken.

    **C** We went out to eat at Jenns restaurant.

    **(D)** The boat's motor was broken.

Tip: If you don't know the answer at all, make an educated guess.

**End of Section.**

# SECTION 3

# Section 3: The OSSLT Testing Lab

You have two booklets to complete, and each has a specific time limit:

| | |
|---|---|
| Booklet 1 (Reading and Writing) | 75 minutes |
| Break | 15 minutes |
| Booklet 2 (Reading and Writing) | 75 minutes |
| Questionnaire (Booklet 2) | 10 minutes |

The test contains both operational items (those that count toward your score) and field-test items (those that are embedded in the test for trial purposes and do not count toward your score; they account for less than 20% of the allotted testing time).

The operational component of the test consists of

- 31 multiple-choice reading items related to five reading selections;
- four open-response items related to three of the five reading selections;
- eight multiple-choice writing items;
- two short open-response writing tasks; and
- two long open-response writing tests (a series of paragraphs expressing an opinion and a news report).

Answers are filled in on the Student Answer Sheet and written responses are written in the *Test Booklet*.

The total number of points possible on the OSSLT is 81. There are rubrics which include score codes that are converted to score points. Each question is scored differently:

- multiple-choice: correct = 1; incorrect or blank = 0
- open-response reading: 0-3 points depending on the quality of the response
- short-writing prompts: 0-2 points for conventions and 0-3 points for topic development
- long-writing prompts: 0-4 points for conventions and 0-6 points for topic development

These points are converted to a score based on the relationship between your overall ability in reading and writing to your performance on individual items. The score will lie somewhere between 200 and 400 points. You must achieve a score of 300 points to pass, which is approximately 70% of the score points available on the test.

---

Information found on EQAO website. Check frequently for accuracy and updates.

# OSSLT Test: timed assessment of reading and writing skills

Hey. My name is Alex and I am from Peterborough. I took the OSSLT last year and the biggest hurdle for me was that it was timed. I knew it was going to be timed, but I never practiced dividing my time up before. I did a lot of practice developing my skills for the test but I didn't work on time-management skills. I found that I was so focussed on doing everything right and checking and double-checking my work that I ran out of time before I had finished the first booklet. So, when it came time to work on the second booklet, I looked at all the tasks in it first and made sure to divide my time between all of them. I actually finished five minutes early and then went back over the test booklet to do a thorough check and proof-read.

Hey there. I'm Zach and I'm from Woodstock. I had to get used to the answer sheet. In all my practice I just circled the answers right on the practice sheet. However, in the test all the multiple-choice answers had to be marked in circles on an answer sheet. The multiple-choice questions are marked using a computer, so it is important to mark your answer in the correct line on your answer sheet. It doesn't hurt to double-check before filling in the circle to make sure you are marking the right one. Cut out the Student Answer Sheet on the next page so you can use it to practice when you complete the practice test.

*The OSSLT Literacy Lab*

# Student Answer Sheet
Sample Test Booklets

## BOOKLET 1

### Section A
1. Ⓐ ● Ⓒ Ⓓ
2. Ⓐ Ⓑ ● Ⓓ
3. Ⓐ Ⓑ Ⓒ ●
4. ● Ⓑ Ⓒ Ⓓ
5. Ⓐ ● Ⓒ Ⓓ
6. Respond in booklet.

### Section B
1. Ⓐ Ⓑ ● Ⓓ
2. Ⓐ ● Ⓒ Ⓓ
3. ● Ⓑ Ⓒ Ⓓ
4. Ⓐ ● Ⓒ Ⓓ
5. Ⓐ Ⓑ Ⓒ ●

### Section C
1. ● Ⓑ Ⓒ Ⓓ
2. Ⓐ Ⓑ ● Ⓓ
3. Ⓐ Ⓑ ● Ⓓ
4. Ⓐ Ⓑ Ⓒ ●
5. Ⓐ ● Ⓒ Ⓓ
6. Ⓐ ● Ⓒ Ⓓ
7. Respond in booklet.

### Section D
1. Respond in booklet.

### Section E
1. Respond in booklet.

### Section F
1. ● Ⓑ Ⓒ Ⓓ
2. Ⓐ ● Ⓒ Ⓓ
3. Ⓐ Ⓑ Ⓒ ●
4. ● Ⓑ Ⓒ Ⓓ
5. Ⓐ Ⓑ ● Ⓓ
6. Ⓐ ● Ⓒ Ⓓ
7. Respond in booklet.

### End of *Booklet 1*

## BOOKLET 2

### Section G
1. Respond in booklet.

### Section H
1. Ⓐ ● Ⓒ Ⓓ
2. Ⓐ Ⓑ Ⓒ ●
3. Ⓐ Ⓑ ● Ⓓ
4. ● Ⓑ Ⓒ Ⓓ

### Section I
1. Ⓐ Ⓑ ● Ⓓ
2. ● Ⓑ Ⓒ Ⓓ
3. Ⓐ ● Ⓒ Ⓓ
4. Ⓐ Ⓑ ● Ⓓ
5. Ⓐ ● Ⓒ Ⓓ
6. Ⓐ Ⓑ Ⓒ ●
7. Ⓐ Ⓑ ● Ⓓ
8. ● Ⓑ Ⓒ Ⓓ
9. Ⓐ Ⓑ Ⓒ ●

### Section J
1. Ⓐ ● Ⓒ Ⓓ
2. Ⓐ Ⓑ ● Ⓓ
3. Ⓐ Ⓑ Ⓒ ●
4. Ⓐ ● Ⓒ Ⓓ
5. Ⓐ ● Ⓒ Ⓓ
6. Respond in booklet.
7. Respond in booklet.

### Section K
1. Respond in booklet.

### Section L
1. Ⓐ Ⓑ Ⓒ ●
2. Ⓐ ● Ⓒ Ⓓ
3. ● Ⓑ Ⓒ Ⓓ
4. ● Ⓑ Ⓒ Ⓓ
5. Ⓐ Ⓑ Ⓒ ●
6. Ⓐ ● Ⓒ Ⓓ

## Student Questionnaire

### Section M
1. Ⓨ Ⓝ
2. Ⓨ Ⓝ
3. Ⓨ Ⓝ
4. Ⓨ Ⓝ
5. Ⓨ Ⓝ
6. Ⓨ Ⓝ
7. Ⓨ Ⓝ
8. Ⓨ Ⓝ
9. Ⓨ Ⓝ

### End of Test

Print Student Name: _____

_____

Student Signature: _____

# SECTION 2

THE OSSLT RUBRIC LAB

# Rubric Lab: scoring criteria, samples and exemplars

. . . . . . . . . . . . . . . . . . . . . . . . . . . . . . . . . . . . . . . . . . . .

**The Rubric Lab showcases the scoring criteria and exemplars so students can learn how they will be marked on the OSSLT.**

# Rubric Lab

In the Rubric Lab you will find the scoring criteria based on the EQAO expectations at the time of publication. These expectation can change, so please check back to their website frequently at www.eqao.com

Besides rubrics, you will find possible student answers for each code.

Student answers are indicated by this less formal font. An exercise you can do with your students is to show them a sample student answer and to have students assign the answer a code using the rubric. This allows students to really focus on what is required of them to obtain a particular code. For example, they may see that if they add one more specific detail, their score could go from one code up to another.

For New Reports and Long-Writing, conventions are scored separately with their own set of codes. Exemplars are not provided for conventions in this resource, however, asking students to score existing exemplars in this resource using the rubric is a great way for them to understand how conventions play a role in the OSSLT.

# Open-Response

| Code | Descriptor |
|---|---|
| Blank | **nothing written or drawn in the space provided** |
| Illegible | **response is illegible or is a comment on the task (e.g., I don't know.)** |
| Off topic/ Incorrect | **response is off-topic, irrelevant or incorrect**<br><br>a typical off-topic response provides no information from the reading selection.<br><br>A typical irrelevant response comments on the reading selection or simply restates the question.<br><br>A typical incorrect response<br>   - provides an answer based on a misunderstanding of the question AND/OR the ideas in the reading selection.<br>OR<br>   - provides a general comment about the selection. |
| Code 10 | • **response indicates minimal reading comprehension**<br>• **response provides minimal or irrelevant ideas and information from the reading selection**<br><br>The response provides information with<br>   - no support or details from the selection<br>OR<br>   - a retelling of events in the reading selection<br>OR<br>   - irrelevant details from the selection |
| Code 20 | • **response indicates some reading comprehension**<br>• **response provides vague ideas and information from the reading selection; it may include irrelevant ideas and information from the reading selection**<br><br>The response provides a response with a vague explanation. The response often requires the reader to make connections. |
| Code 30 | • **response indicates considerable reading comprehension**<br>• **response provides accurate, specific and relevant ideas and information from the reading selection** |

# Open-Response Exemplars

Based on the Open-Response Rubric on page 83, here are some possible student answers for each code for the Open-Response question found on page 80 in *The OSSLT Literacy Lab Student Workbook*.

**Code 30:** Are volunteer hours a useful part of the high school experience?

I think volunteer hours are a really useful part of the high school experience. As Toronto Grade 11 student Leah Giles said in the article, "You can be a part of an organization that actually changes something." Being forced to do volunteer hours makes students give of their time and help an organization that they may otherwise have overlooked. When students graduate, they have 40 hours of community service that they can put onto their resumes. If you complete the hours in high school, you can apply to more scholarships since many require volunteer hours.

**Code 20:** Are volunteer hours a useful part of the high school experience?

I think doing 40 hours of community service is way too much! Teenagers have lots going on, like part-time jobs and homework. How can we fit 40 hours in too? I don't want to do 40 hours. No way! I'm not going to. The website sounds cool. I hope I can try it. It might be kinda fun. I hope I get to meet the surprise celebrities too. That would definitely be cool.

**Code 10:** Are volunteer hours a useful part of the high school experience?

Leah is a weird name. It's weird that there's an 'h' on the end. I don't know why it's there when you don't say it. I like the picture of her hair. She looks stylish. They're making a website about volunteering. She's visiting a charity. I don't know what 'daunting' means.

# Short-Writing Task

| Code | Descriptor |
|---|---|
| Blank | nothing written or drawn in the space provided |
| Illegible | response is illegible or is a comment on the task (e.g., I don't know.) |
| Off topic/ Incorrect | response is off-topic, irrelevant or incorrect<br><br>A typical off-topic response is not related to the topic.<br><br>A typical irrelevant response comments on the topic or simply restates the questions. |
| Code 10 | response is not developed or is developed with irrelevant ideas and information |
| Code 20 | response is developed with vague ideas and information; it may contain some irrelevant ideas and information |
| Code 30 | response is developed with clear, specific and relevant ideas and information |

# Short-Writing Task Exemplars

Based on the Short-Writing Rubric on page 85, here are some possible student answers for each code for the Short-Writing question found on page 85 of *The OSSLT Literacy Lab Student Workbook.*

**Code 30:** What is your favourite season of the year? Use specific details to explain why.

My favourite season of the year is fall. I really like it because there is so much beauty to look at during the fall season. I love how the leaves on the trees turn colour. The reds and oranges are so pretty. I like to take photographs and I enjoy taking photographs of the changing fall leaves. I also like it that the weather is still pretty warm. It doesn't feel too cold outside and I like that occasionally there may still even be a hot day. My favourite holiday, Thanksgiving, is in the fall and I love to spend time with my family and eat delicious food. The best part of the fall, though, is Halloween! I love getting dressed up and getting lots of treats such as chocolate and candy.

**Code 20:** What is your favourite season of the year? Use specific details to explain why.

If I had to choose a favourite season I would say summer. I like it because we don't have to go to school. I don't like school, but my brother does. He gets upset when summer comes because he can't go to school. My mom's favourite season is winter because she likes the cold. My favourite thing to have for dinner is spaghetti. I also like summer because I get to sleep in and I get to eat lots. The summer is really hot too and I like that. I don't like the cold.

**Code 10:** What is your favourite season of the year? Use specific details to explain why.

I don't really like any season. My mom says we get to go to Florida this winter and I'm looking forward to that. I like to play at the beach. I hope it doesn't rain a lot. I get to miss 5 days of school for the trip. I want to take lots of pictures. I want to go swimming too.

The OSSLT Literacy Lab Answer Key and Teacher's Guide

87

# Writing a News Report

| Code | Descriptor |
|------|-----------|
| **Blank** | The pages are blank with nothing written or drawn in the space provided. |
| **Illegible** | The response is illegible, or irrelevant to the prompt. |
| **Off topic** | The response is off topic. |
| **Code 10** | The response is related to the headline and/or photo but is not a news report. **OR** The response is a news report related to the headline and/or photo. It identifies an event, but provides no supporting details, or provides details that are unrelated to the event. There is no evidence of organization. |
| **Code 20** | The response is related to the headline and/or photo but only partly in the form of a news report. **OR** The response is a news report related to the headline and/or photo, but the focus on an event is unclear or inconsistent. There is insufficient supporting details: too few or repetitious. There is limited evidence of organization. |
| **Code 30** | The response is a news report related to the headline and photo with a clear focus on the event. There are insufficient and/or vague supporting details or the connection of the details to the event is not always clear. There is evidence of organization, but lapses distract from the overall communication. |
| **Code 40** | The response is a news report related to the headline and photo with a clear and consistent focus on the event. There are sufficient supporting details, however, only some are specific. The organization is mechanical and any lapses do not distract from the overall communication. |
| **Code 50** | The response is a news report related to the headline and photo with a clear and consistent focus on the event. There are sufficient specific supporting details to develop the news report. The organization is logical. |
| **Code 60** | The response is a news report related to the headline and photo with a clear and consistent focus on an event. There are sufficient specific supporting details, which are thoughtfully chosen to develop the news report. The organization is coherent demonstrating a thoughtful progression of ideas. |

# News Report Sample Answer

Sample News Report from page 86 of *The OSSLT Literacy Lab Student Workbook.*

### Students Save Local Dog Park

Rose Dog Park is saved! Students from St. Xanthum Elementary School celebrated when they heard the official word from City Hall. Rose Dog Park would not be closed and would remain open for countless dogs and their owners to enjoy for many years to come. St. Xanthum student Claire Jones said, "We are so happy because all of our effort has paid off!"

The idea to save the park started when local student Emily Smit saw a sign posted in the park which said that the park would be closing because there wasn't enough money at City Hall to maintain the park. Emily was really upset because she would no longer be able to enjoy the park with her dog, Poppy. That night, Emily talked it over with her parents and they said she should come up with a solution to save the park. The next day, Emily talked it over with some classmates and they too wanted to save the park. They discussed the problem and their solution was to have a bake sale to raise money to keep the park open.

Emily and the other students baked for days in preparation. "It was a lot of hard work!" said Emily, "but it was worth it in the end!" They advertised in the local paper and their bake sale was a success! They sold over 1000 cupcakes and some people that came to the fundraiser donated money too. They raised enough money to keep the park open! Emily and some of her classmates gave the money to City Hall and the mayor said, "We are so thankful for Emily and the students of St. Xanthum Elementary School. Through their hard work, the dogs of this city can run free and be happy!"

As shown in the article, the dogs can now run free and enjoy the park. Poppy is pictured on the far left running with her dog friends. Thanks to the hard work of the students of St. Xanthum Elementary School, the dogs don't have to worry about the park closing anytime soon.

# Long-Writing Topic Development

| Code | Descriptor |
|---|---|
| **Blank** | The pages are blank with nothing written or drawn in the space provided. |
| **Illegible** | The response is illegible, or irrelevant to the prompt. |
| **Off topic** | The response is off topic. |
| **Code 10** | The response is related to the prompt but does not express an opinion. **OR** The response expresses an opinion with no supporting details or provides details unrelated to the opinion. There is no evidence of organization. |
| **Code 20** | The response is related to the prompt, but only part of the response expresses and supports an opinion. **OR** The response is related to the prompt, and expresses and supports an opinion, but the opinion is unclear or inconsistent. There are insufficient supporting details: too few or repetitious. There is limited evidence of organization. |
| **Code 30** | The response is related to the prompt and expresses a clear opinion. There are insufficient and/or vague supporting details or the connection of the details to the opinion is not always clear. There is evidence of organization, but lapses distract from the overall communication. |
| **Code 40** | The response is related to the prompt. A clear and consistent opinion is developed with sufficient supporting details, however only some are specific. The organization is mechanical and any lapses do not distract from the overall communication. |
| **Code 50** | The response is related to the prompt. A clear and consistent opinion is developed with sufficient specific supporting details. The organization is logical. |
| **Code 60** | The response is related to the assigned prompt. A clear and consistent opinion is developed with sufficient specific supporting details that are thoughtfully chosen. The organization is coherent demonstrating a thoughtful progression of ideas. |

# Long-Writing Task Exemplars

Based on the Long-Writing Rubric on page 90, here are some possible student answers for each code for the Long-Writing question found on page 95 of *The OSSLT Literacy Lab Student Workbook.*

**Code 60:** Is the use of technology making teenagers less social?

I think that the use of technology is making teenagers less social. The first reason is that technology isolates teenagers. By being isolated, teenagers spend less time with each other. The second reason is that technology encourages interaction through an interface, rather than in person. Teens interact with the piece of technology rather than speaking directly with a friend. The third reason is that technology can be really exciting and can distract teenagers, which leads them to withdraw and focus on the technology rather than hanging out with friends. Teens end up living in a virtual world rather than spending time in the real world.

When teens use technology, they are often by themselves, alone in their rooms. This has a tendency to isolate teenagers and eliminates healthy interaction with other teens. Rather than hanging out in person, teens text from a distance. Teenagers spend most of their free time using technology by themselves. For example, the purpose of texting is to communicate over a distance rather than discuss in person. Another example is when teenagers wear earphones to listen to music. This shuts out contact with other people. By its very nature, technology isolates which makes teens less social. If teens aren't interacting with each other, than they are being less social. Technology is always advancing and teenagers stay on top of these advances. For example, there is a new type of technology which enables you to wear glasses which are really a computer. Teens see the world through the lens of a computer. Rather than interacting with people directly, teens interact through a computer interface. This encourages a mask of humanity, but really means that teens aren't interacting with each other.

Technology can be really exciting for teenagers. For example, when a new game comes out, teens spend hours playing the game and don't spend time with friends or family. The enticing technology draws teenagers away from contact with others and instead, teens spend time in a virtual world rather than reality.

Technology does have its benefits, but encouraging the development of social skills in teenagers is not one of them. In fact, technology encourages teens to be less social. Teens spend time texting, rather than talking face-to-face with each other. Teens stay on top of trends and wear new technology, like glasses with a computer built into them. Unfortunately, teens interact through the lens of a computer, rather than talking with their friends in person. Finally, teens can spend days holed up in their rooms using technology without interacting with anyone at all. This is especially true when a new piece of technology comes out. Teenagers should be social, not constricted by technology.

**Code 50:** Is the use of technology making teenagers less social?

The use of technology is not making teenagers less social. In fact, the use of technology is making teenagers more social. According to a leading researcher in the field of psychology, "teenagers use technology to enhance interactions with their peers." Teens use technology as a tool for communication.

The use of technology as a tool for communication can be demonstrated by video games. Teens hang out at each other's houses playing video games for hours on end. When playing games, teens interact with each other, laugh, share meals, and talk about the game. Video games are a bonding moment. There's a club that's run at a local high school which promotes the use of video games. Teachers support this club because they say that it is bonding time for the teens. By using the technology of video games, teens become more social.

The use of technology as a tool for communication can also be demonstrated by the internet. When teens have to work on a project at school, they often use the internet as a research tool. When surfing the internet for a project, teens often do this together and talk about what they are researching. If teens do spend time surfing the internet, they often do this just to get facts about what's happening in the world so they can stay current with pop culture. They use this information when bonding with their friends to share what they learned. Using the internet promotes social interaction with teens.

Finally, the use of technology as a tool for communication can be demonstrated by phones. Some people say teens text too much, but isn't this a way of being social? You really are just talking with your friends. Usually conversations had by using a phone are just a means to arrange meeting up in person.

Technology is a great tool which aids social interaction. Technology is out there—it's everywhere and teens have embraced it. They use technology as a tool to develop positive social interactions with friends and to build relationships. Video games, the internet, and phones are some tools which teens use to establish connections with friends.

**Code 40:** Is the use of technology making teenagers less social?

Teenagers in general can be awkward and anti-social, but the use of technology is making teenagers even more awkward and anti-social than normal. When one used to think of a teenager, one would think of someone with acne and braces. The modern image of teenager remains the same, with the addition of headphones and a hoodie. Teenagers withdraw when technology is around, and that makes for a less social teen.

When teens plug in to technology, they totally forget about their surroundings and forget about having a conversation! Teenagers even want to plug in during class and by doing so, they isolate from everyone else. Teenagers are socially awkward to begin with, and by using technology, they become even more awkward. Having a conversation on Facebook is not the same as having a conversation in person. Teens today have lost the ability to have a meaningful conversation. Today's technology encourages isolation and awkwardness. You can't listen to your ipod with someone else. It's designed to cut everything else out and to make you focus on what you are listening to. And what is the number one company today? Yes, Apple. Everyone is doing it! Teens love fads, and wearing a ipod is cool. Having a fancy phone is cool. If it's cool, teenagers will do it just so that they can fit in.

The use of the internet also promotes a teen society which is not social. When people use the internet, they are surfing the web alone, sometimes for hours at a time. Rather than hang out with friends, teens want to surf the web. Some people shop on-line, which is another example of how teens are less social. In the past, teens would hang out with their friends at the mall. Not anymore! Teens shop on-line now. In the past, teens would date people in their classes and get to know them through having a conversation with them. Not anymore! In today's modern world, teens hardly date at all and instead spend time at home playing video games. This is not a way to promote a healthy social development.

I think teens are less social because of technology. Video games, ipods and the internet are three pieces of technology which tend to make teenagers be less social. Before this type of technology was around, teenagers spent all their free time with their friends. Now teens are choosing to spend their free time in isolation playing with their technology.

**Code 30:** Is the use of technology making teenagers less social?

Technology is really important because we use computers in class all the time. Even though technology is important, it has a downside. It's making teenagers less social. This is not a good thing because teenagers should be social and hang out with each other. People love technology so much they line up for days just to get the new phone. I should know because I did it! When you get a new piece of technology, you just hang out with it instead of hanging out with your friends. My sister spends hours and hours just texting from her room and she doesn't see anybody at all. And, she's getting addicted. She even wants to text during dinner! My mom says, "put the phone away!" Even though my sister spends a lot of time texting, she doesn't hang out with friends much. I don't hang out with friends much either because I like to go home and play videogames and watch tv. I can spend hours watching tv. I guess if I watched tv with a friend I would be more social. Maybe I should invite a friend over and try to be more social.

**Code 20:** Is the use of technology making teenagers less social?

Teenagers are less social now because of technology. Teenagers like to spend time talking on the phone, but they don't hang out in person. I don't spend as much time with my friends as I used to. We just talk on the phone now or text. It's easier and I don't have to bother going to their houses, catching a ride, or walking over there. I don't really talk to too many people, but when I do, I just send a text. When my friends want to get together they just text me and I meet them. We like to hang out and go see movies. We went to go see "Runner" on Friday and it was really scary. We spent hours together. Then we went to go get something to eat after that. A bunch of us went and we had a good time. If we didn't text using technology, then we wouldn't have got together. Technology is making us more social. When we are in school we just sit in front of a computer. We don't talk to each other and we just enter codes into the computer in my programming class. It's pretty boring, but we don't look too social because we're all just sitting, staring at a computer. Using the computers makes us pretty unsocial.

**Code 10:** Is the use of technology making teenagers less social?

I like to hang out with my friends and play video games. Our favourite game to play is Dragon's Breath which is really hard to beat. We spend hours playing that game at my house. When my friends come over to my house to play games, I am being social. We have dances at school and I go to those sometimes. It's fun to dance and get dressed up. I also like to hang out with my friends in the caf over lunch. Sometimes they tease me because I like to eat two hamburgers for lunch every day. It's good. I also like to hang out with my friends after school. We go to Homework Club and I can get help on my math homework. I did really great on my last math test and when I got it signed my dad was really happy about it. He said I did good.

# News Report and Long-Writing Conventions

| Code | Descriptor |
|---|---|
| **Code 10** | There is insufficient evidence to assess the use of conventions.<br>**OR**<br>Errors in conventions interfere with communication. |
| **Code 20** | Errors in conventions distract from communication. |
| **Code 30** | Errors in conventions do not distract from communication. |
| **Code 40** | Control of conventions is evident in written work. |

# SECTION 3

THE OSSLT LESSON LAB

# Lesson Lab: sample lessons and differentiated learning ideas

· · · · · · · · · · · · · · · · · · · · · · · · · · · · · · · · · · · · · · · · · · · ·

The Lessons Lab offers five unique lessons to reinforce skills presented in *The OSSLT Student Workbook.* Use these lessons as they are, or modify them to meet the needs of your students.

# Lesson 1: Topic Verses Main Idea

1. Explain that the topic is the subject of the paragraph whereas the main idea deals with the point, thought or opinion being expressed.

2. One strategy for determining the main point is to turn the first sentence into a question and then read the paragraph for the answer.

3. Use page 10 in *The OSSLT Literacy Lab Student Workbook* as an example.

   Turn the first sentence into a question:
   > *What variety of purposes and activities does Algonquin Provincial Park serve?*

   Answers found in the paragraph:
   > *tourism*
   >
   > *interpretation centre*
   >
   > *historic structures*
   >
   > *museums*
   >
   > *activities such a day hiking and cross-country skiing*
   >
   > *conservation*
   >
   > *research*
   >
   > *industry (such as logging)*

4. Ask students to do the same procedure for the information paragraph found on page 15 in *The OSSLT Literacy Lab Student Workbook*

**Differentiated Learning Idea**

• Ask students to watch a TV commercial, distinguishing between topic and main idea.

For example: ask students to watch an XYZ detergent commercial.

Topic: detergent
Main idea: XYZ detergent gets out difficult stains better than ABC detergent.

# Lesson 2: Organizing Paragraphs

**Differentiated Learning Idea**

• Ask students to find a television show and verbally explain how it is organized.

For example: a how-to show is organized by steps, and a historical documentary or biography may be organized chronologically

1. Discuss various ways a paragraph can be organized. For example, chronological order, general to specific, specific to general, cause and effect and compare and contrast.

2. Ask students to find a sample text that represents one type of organization and write 3-4 sentences defending why.

# Lesson 3: News Report

1. Discuss the questions answered in most news reports such as Who? What? Where? When? How? and Why?

2. Ask students to choose a news report and answer the questions.

**Differentiated Learning Idea**

Ask students to watch a news broadcast on TV and verbally answer the questions Who? What? Where? When? How? and Why?

# Lesson 4: Dialogue

**Differentiated Learning Idea**

- Ask students to watch a play, TV show etc. and verbally identify who is involved in the dialogue.

1. Discuss the meaning of the word "dialogue."

2. Ask students to find a passage that involves characters, and ask them to rewrite the passage as a dialogue.

# Lesson 5: Graphic Text

1. Ask students to find a schedule such as a bus, recreational or class schedule.

2. Ask students to recreate the schedule using different graphical representations and organization.

**Differentiated Learning Idea**

- Ask students to find a schedule and make suggestions how it could be reorganized/ represented.

# SECTION 4

**THE OSSLT HANDOUT LAB**

# Handout Lab: classroom handouts featuring a variety of topics and tips

· · · · · · · · · · · · · · · · · · · · · · · · · · · · · · · · · · · · · · · · · · · · · · · · · · · · ·

The Handout Lab is a unique section of this resource. Any school that has purchased this book may photocopy the following pages for student use within the school. Pick and choose appropriate handouts for differentiated learning, or use this section for extra practice in particular skills. Or, use all the handouts with all of your students. The choice is yours.

# OSSLT Glossary of Terms

**Selection**    A **selection** is the reading passage provided that you will use as the basis for writing your answers.

**Task**    The **task** is the activity you have to complete. Instructions will be given. For example, you may be instructed to develop your main idea using supporting details from the selection.

**Response**    The **response** is the written answer you provide.

**Length**    The **length** is how long your response is. The amount of lines provided is a good guide as to what **length** your response should be.

**Rough Notes**    There is a space on the test to brainstorm ideas or make graphic organizers. This is referred to as the **rough notes**. This area is NOT scored.

**Conventions**    **Conventions** are things such as spelling, grammar, sentence structure and punctuation. Good use of **conventions** makes your response easier to understand.

**Section**    The literacy test is organized into chunks of activities referred to as **sections**.

# Personal Dictionary

Write down words you encounter that you don't know the meaning of. Find the meanings and fill it in.

| Word | Meaning |
|------|---------|
|      |         |
|      |         |
|      |         |
|      |         |
|      |         |
|      |         |
|      |         |
|      |         |
|      |         |
|      |         |
|      |         |
|      |         |
|      |         |
|      |         |

**STUDENT HANDOUT FOR *THE OSSLT LITERACY LAB***

# Transition Words and Punctuation Rules

The following list provides examples of some common and useful transitional words and phrases.

**cause and effect**: consequently, therefore, accordingly, as a result, because, for this reason, hence, thus

**sequence**: furthermore, in addition, moreover, first, second, third, finally, again, also, and, besides, further, in the first place, last, likewise, next, then, too

**comparison or contrast**: similarly, also, in the same way, likewise, although, at the same time, but, conversely, even so, however, in contrast, nevertheless, nonetheless, notwithstanding, on the contrary, otherwise, still, yet

**example**: for example, for instance, in fact, indeed, of course, specifically, that is, to illustrate

**reason**: for this purpose, for this reason, to this end, with this object time or location: nearby, above, adjacent to, below, beyond, farther on, here, opposite to, there, to the south, before, after, later, afterward, immediately, in the meantime, meanwhile, now, since, soon, then, while

## Punctuation Rules

**Coordinating Conjunctions** (and, but, or, yet, so):
Put a comma before these conjunctions. (Don't use them at the beginning of a sentence in more formal writing.)
*Example: The library has already closed, but my friend has not arrived yet.*

**Correlative Conjunctions** (These have two parts: either/or):
Put a comma before the second part if it connects two independent clauses (complete sentences).
*Example: Todd is not only an outstanding student, but he is also an accomplished athlete.*

You don't need a comma if it only connects words or phrases.
*Example: Karen is not only an outstanding student but also an accomplished athlete.*

**Transitional Words and Phrases**:
Put a comma after these if they are at the beginning of a sentence.
*Example: I like to sing. Specifically, I enjoy modern music.*

# Basic Sentence Structure

**The sentence is basic to language. It expresses a complete thought and consists of a subject and a predicate.**

- The subject is the person, animal, thing or abstract concept that is the focus of the sentence.
- The predicate is the action or state of being the subject is taking. Here is an example:

> The person walked down the street.
>
> subject: person
>
> predicate: walked down the street

**There are two common mistakes with composing sentences.**

- The sentence is incomplete. It is missing either the subject or the predicate. Here are some examples:

> The very young boy. *(no predicate: what did the very young boy do?)*
>
> Rolling down the hill. *(no subject: who was rolling down the hill?)*
>
> Generally feeling lousy. *(no subject: who was generally feeling lousy?)*

- There are too many complete thoughts. In this case, sentences can run into each other. Here are some examples:

> The young boy kicked the boy he loved to play soccer.
>
> It was a hot summer I didn't like the heat, my mother was mad.

**When you compose your sentences, make sure that you are using complete, well-constructed sentences.**

# Using Capital Letters

| When to use capital letters | Examples |
| --- | --- |
| First word of a sentence | **S**he walked down to the store after school. |
| The pronoun "I" | **I** am glad that **I** am going to the dance. |
| Proper nouns such as names and nicknames of particular persons and characters | **S**heila **C**opps, **D**oreen **W**ilkinson, **J**effry **T**yler |
| Titles that come before particular persons and characters | **Q**ueen Elizabeth II, **D**octor Phillips |
| Names of specific places such as planets, countries, counties, seas, streets etc. | **B**ancroft, **L**ake **S**imcoe, **Y**onge **S**treet |
| Names of nationalities | **S**cottish, **C**anadian, **M**exican |
| Names of businesses, buildings and schools | **P**arliament **B**uildings, **A**nywhere **S**econdary **S**chool |
| Days, months and holidays | **T**hanksgiving, **T**uesday, **A**pril |
| Titles such as books, movies, plays and magazines | *Arctic Air,* *The OSSLT Literacy Lab* |
| Acronyms | **CSA** (Canadian Space Agency) **TV** (teleivision) |

# Common Punctuation

| Symbol | Punctuation | Example of Use |
|---|---|---|
| **.** | A **period** is used at the end of a sentence or with abbreviations. | She didn't know where to get driving lessons.<br>M.P. (Member of Parliament) |
| **!** | An **exclamation mark** is used to indicate strong feelings or a raised voice at the end of a sentence. | Stop!<br>Hurry up and get help! |
| **?** | A **question mark** is used to indicate a query. | What is your name? |
| **" "** | **Quotation marks** are used to show what someone said. | The student asked, "How is the test marked?" |
| **,** | A **comma** is used to indicate a pause, to set off a phrase or to separate items in a series. | My favourite sports are soccer, basketball, rugby and golf. |
| **'** | An **apostrophe** is used to show possession or to represent missing letters in contractions. | Jesse's sister was coming to town.<br>Don't tell me what to do. |
| **( )** | **Parentheses** are used to set off less important details such as an afterthought or a personal comment. | Seth (the student who used to be my neighbour) gave a speech at school today. |
| **:** | A **colon** is used to introduce a list or is used in time. | We can see many things in the night sky: the moon, stars, planets, comets and satellites.<br>It was 10:30 in the morning. |
| **;** | A **semicolon** is used to join two related sentences or used to separate items in a series that have commas. | You did your best; now let's hope you pass the test.<br>People came from Edmonton, Alberta; Sharon, Ontario; and Halifax, Nova Scotia. |
| **-** | A **hyphen** is used to divide a word or used in compound words. | Make sure to double-check your answers. |
| **—** | A **dash** is used to connect groups of words to other groups of words in order to emphasize a point. | Years ago—when nobody had electricity—water was often pumped by hand. |
| **...** | An **ellipse** is used to indicate a pause or that the thought or quote was cut off. | "I really wanted to go to the party...but my parents said that I couldn't." |

STUDENT HANDOUT FOR *THE OSSLT LITERACY LAB*

# You Don't "Say"
## (or words to use instead of "said")

| | | | |
|---|---|---|---|
| added | addressed | advised | agreed |
| announced | answered | assured | babbled |
| begged | blurted | called | cautioned |
| cheered | chided | chuckled | claimed |
| commanded | confessed | confided | cried |
| declared | demanded | described | disagreed |
| divulged | echoed | exclaimed | explained |
| gasped | greeted | groaned | guessed |
| hinted | hissed | hollered | hypothesized |
| imitated | implied | inquired | insisted |
| interjected | interrupted | jeered | joked |
| mentioned | moaned | mumbled | murmured |
| muttered | nagged | noted | objected |
| observed | offered | ordered | piped |
| pleaded | pondered | proclaimed | protested |
| queried | questioned | quipped | ranted |
| reasoned | recalled | reported | responded |
| screamed | scolded | shouted | shrieked |
| sighed | snapped | sneered | snickered |
| sniffed | sobbed | spoke | sputtered |
| stammered | stated | suggested | surmised |
| taunted | teased | tempted | theorized |
| threatened | told | urged | uttered |
| volunteered | vowed | wailed | warned |
| whimpered | whined | whispered | wondered |

# Checklist for Writing a Series of Paragraphs Expressing an Opinion

- ☐ My opinion is clearly stated in the introductory paragraph.
- ☐ I have written three (3) or more paragraphs.
- ☐ I have a clear introduction, body and conclusion.
- ☐ I have included reasons or examples that support my opinion.
- ☐ I have used complete sentences.
- ☐ I have linked ideas.
- ☐ I have used correct grammar, spelling and punctuation.

# Checklist for Writing Short-Writing Tasks

- ☐ I clearly stated my main idea in my opening sentence.
- ☐ I have included reasons and details to support my response.
- ☐ My paragraph is logically organized.
- ☐ My paragraph makes sense and addresses the question.
- ☐ I have used complete sentences.
- ☐ I have proof-read for correct spelling, grammar and punctuation.

# Checklist for Writing a News Report

- ☐ I have connected the headline AND the picture in my writing.
- ☐ I have answered the questions Who? What? Where? When? Why? and How?
- ☐ I have included at least one direct and indirect quote.
- ☐ I have used my imagination to make up participants, events and details to support the headline and picture.
- ☐ I have organized the report in a logical manner, using paragraphs.
- ☐ I  have used complete sentences.
- ☐ I have proof-read for correct spelling, grammar and punctuation.

# General Editing Checklist

☐ My ideas are clear.

☐ My purpose of the writing is clear.

☐ My writing is clear for the intended audience.

☐ My beginning, middle and end are clearly indicated and well-organized.

☐ My main idea is supported with details, illustrations or examples.

☐ My words are understandable and appropriate. They are clearly used.

☐ My language level is appropriate for the subject and audience.

☐ My sentences are varied in both length and structure.

☐ My writing is logical and makes sense.

☐ Conventions of writing such as grammar, punctuation and spelling are used correctly.

# Strategies for Multiple-Choice Questions

- Read each question thoroughly.

- Make sure you know what the question is asking.

- Look at all of the answer choices before answering.

- Pace yourself.

- Mark question numbers that you can't answer and go on to the next question. Return to the skipped questions at the end, even if you simply mark a guess.

- Try to eliminate the ones you are sure are wrong.

- Use context clues, word prefixes, suffixes and roots to make intelligent guesses about unfamiliar words.

- Check your work.

- Don't leave a question blank.

- Always use the process of elimination first.

- Make an educated guess.

- Choose the most precise answer.

- Avoid answers that seem out of context.

# Opinion Topics

- Are famous people treated unfairly by the media?
- Should zoos be eliminated?
- Do children learn best by observing the behaviour of adults and copying it?
- Computers can translate all kinds of languages well. Do children need to learn more languages in the future?
- Do the benefits of study abroad justify the difficulties?
- Do we become used to bad news? Would it be better if more good news was reported?
- Does modern technology make life more convenient, or was life better when technology was simpler?
- Does travel help to promote understanding and communication between countries?
- Should people be forced to retire at age 65?
- Should sports classes be dropped in secondary school so students can concentrate on academic subjects?
- Do you think graduated licensing is a good thing for Ontario drivers?
- Do you think that the mass media, including TV, radio and newspapers, have great influence in shaping people's ideas?
- Are we becoming too dependent on computers?
- What should a government do for a country to become successful?
- Will modern technology such as the internet ever replace the book or the written word as the main source of information?

# Point of View

Point of view in writing lets the reader know whose perspective the story is being told from. When you write a news report, it must be written in third person. What exactly is first, second and third person anyway?

### What is a first person pronoun?
A pronoun that is used when you are referring to yourself.

### What are all the first person pronouns?
I, me, myself, my, mine, we, us, ours and ourself.

### What is a second person pronoun?
A pronoun that is used when you are referring to the person you are talking to.

### What are all the second person pronouns?
you, yours, yourself and yourselves.

### What is a third person pronoun?
A pronoun that is used when you are referring to a person you are talking about.

### What are all the third person pronouns?
he, she, it, him, her, his, himself, herself, itself, they, them, theirs and themselves.

**What this means:**
When writing a news report, remember you aren't writing it from your point of view, so don't use words like "I," "me," "us," etc. (unless inside a direct quote). Instead, use third person pronouns such as "he," "she," "her," "they" etc.

# Graphic Organizer for Information Paragraphs

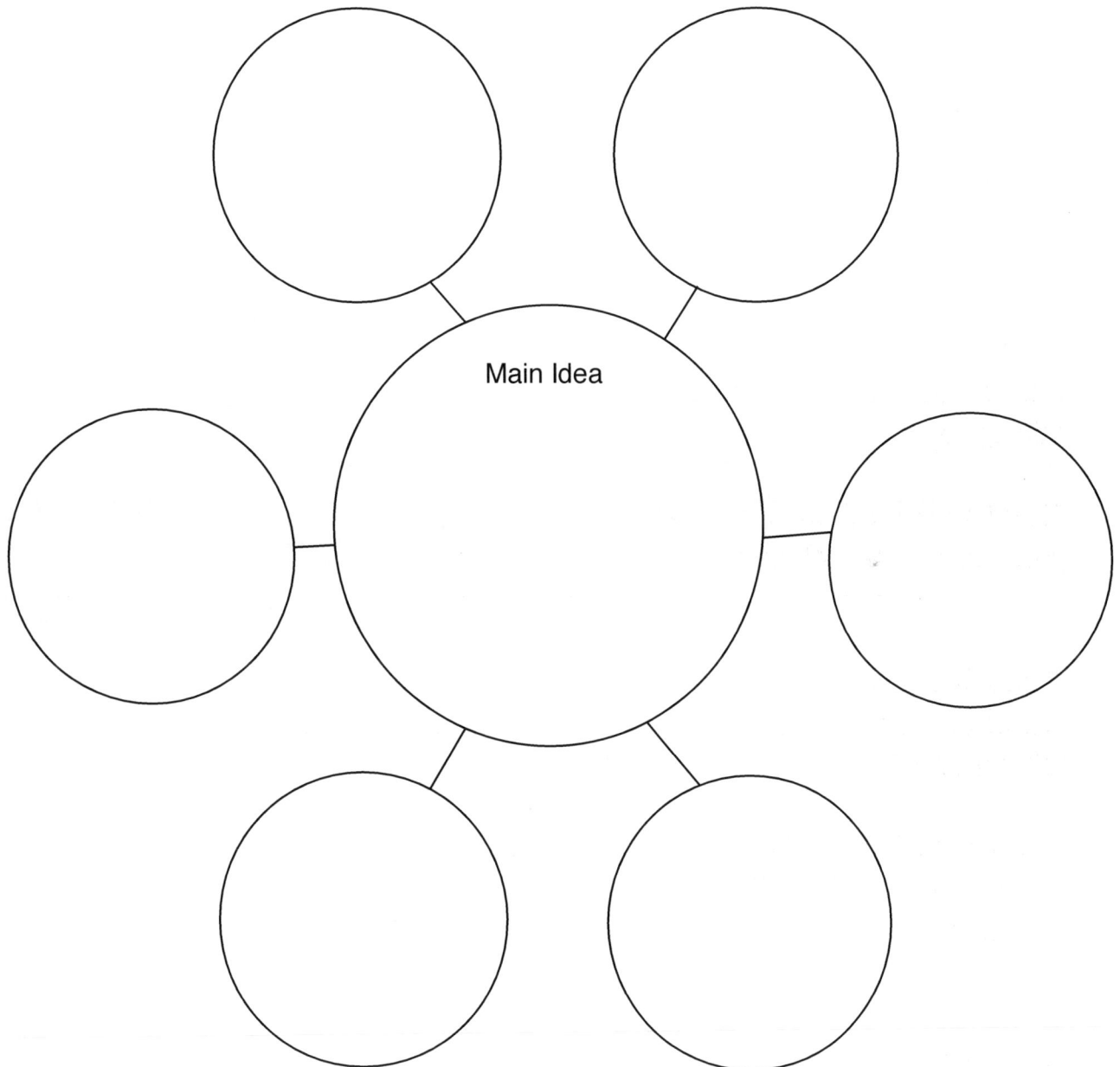

Main Idea

# Graphic Organizer for News Reports

Who?
_____

_____

What?
_____

_____

Where?
_____

_____

When?
_____

_____

Why?
_____

_____

How?
_____

_____

**STUDENT HANDOUT FOR *THE OSSLT LITERACY LAB***

# Commonly Misused Words

| Words | Meaning | In a Sentence |
|---|---|---|
| a lot | to a very great degree; many | I have a lot of friends. |
| allot | give or apportion to | We cannot allot blame to either one. |
| | | |
| their | possessive form of "they" | They moved their car. |
| there | in that place | The park is over there. |
| they're | contraction for "they are" | I know they're coming over today. |
| | | |
| to | toward | I want to go to the park. |
| too | also; very (emphasis) | She is leaving too. |
| two | number following one | I have two brothers. |
| | | |
| its | possessive form of "it" | The dog wagged its tail. |
| it's | contraction for "it is" | I think it's a good store. |
| | | |
| knew | past tense of "know" | I knew he would pass the test. |
| new | fresh, not yet old | I got a new pair of shoes. |
| | | |
| know | to comprehend | I know her from school. |
| no | negative | I have no interest in going there. |
| | | |
| quiet | silent, calm | Please be quiet. |
| quite | very | It was quite a nice day. |
| | | |
| right | correct; opposite of left | He got the answer right. |
| rite | ritual or ceremony | It was a rite of passage. |
| write | to put words on paper | I like to write short answers. |
| | | |
| sight | scene, view, picture | The sight was breathtaking. |
| site | place, location | The building site was by the lake. |
| cite | to document or quote (verb) | She had to cite the source. |
| | | |
| through | finished; into and out of | I managed to get through the day. |
| threw | past tense of "to throw" | He threw the ball. |
| | | |
| your | possessive for "of you" | Remember to bring your pen. |
| you're | contraction for "you are" | I know you're happy. |

# How to Maintain Focus During the Test

Taking the OSSLT requires quite a bit of energy and direct focus for long periods of time. You are probably not used to concentrating so deeply for 75 minutes at a time. It takes stamina and planning to keep on task and to be at your best. Here are some tips to help you focus during the OSSLT:

- Keep up your energy by getting plenty of sleep the night before and eating a well-balanced breakfast.
- If you find your mind is wandering or you are feeling "foggy," change the way you are sitting. Posture affects you physically and mentally. If you improve your posture, you will feel more confident, relaxed and focused. Sometimes a simple shift in the position you are sitting in, or taking a moment to stretch can help you refocus.
- Make sure you interact with the test. You can make notes, draw diagrams or underline important details to help you keep focused on the task.
- Stay calm and focus solely on the single task you are working on. If you are busy worrying, or if you are thinking about the results, you are taking away mental energy you should be using for the activity you are working on.
- Remember to use your break wisely. Try things like stretching, going for a short walk, talking with others, hydrating, using the washroom and eating a healthy snack. These things will help you recharge.
- Don't think about others. This day is about you and the OSSLT. Don't get distracted by paying attention to others in the room.

# Keep Calm—Practice, Prepare and Plan

*"Success is not final, failure is not fatal: it is the courage to continue that counts."*
- Winston Churchill

**There are three possible reasons why students may not pass the OSSLT:**
1. their literacy skills do not meet the expectation of the test;
2. their test-taking skills do not meet the expectation of the test; or
3. a combination of both their literacy and their test-taking skills do not meet the expectation of the test.

**Things to do to help improve your literacy skills**
- read a variety of materials such as newspapers, magazines, blogs, books or short stories
- increase your vocabulary by finding out the meaning of words you don't know
- write a variety of materials such as texts, emails, letters, assignments, news reports and a series of paragraphs expressing an opinion
- use practice materials that simulate the tasks on the OSSLT

**Things to do to help improve your test-taking skills**
- review test-taking strategies
- practice time-management
- use practice materials that simulate the style of questions on the test

**Things that can prevent you from reaching your potential on the day of the test**
- lack of preparation
- anxiety
- not feeling your best (ill, tired or hungry)

Continued on next page ➜

Remember, the test is measuring your performance from just one day in time. It is like taking a small frame out of a long movie. If you do not pass the test, it does not **necessarily** mean that your literacy skills or test-taking skills are below the expectation of the test. It does mean, however, that **on that day**, you did not perform to the standard of the test.

*"You're not obligated to win. You're obligated to keep trying.*
*To the best you can do everyday."*
- Jason Mraz

It's natural to experience some anxiety over a test. However, too much anxiety and pressure can have a negative impact on your performance. So, it is important to keep your anxiety in check. Besides eating well (including a good breakfast), exercising and getting adequate sleep, it is also important to feel prepared and relaxed. Make sure to keep perspective and have a plan for the test **and** the results.

The worst possible outcome is that you do not pass. Although not the preferred result, remember it is not the end of the world. You still have options such as taking the test again or requesting to take the OSSLC (Ontario Secondary School Literacy Course).

Practice, prepare and plan—do your best—but remember to relax and feel confident. You've got this! Whatever the result, you will be okay.

*"It is hard to fail, but it is worse never to have tried to succeed."*
- Theodore Roosevelt

## The OSSLT Literacy Lab

# Student Answer Sheet
## Sample Test Booklets

---

### *BOOKLET 1*

**Section A**

1. Ⓐ Ⓑ Ⓒ Ⓓ
2. Ⓐ Ⓑ Ⓒ Ⓓ
3. Ⓐ Ⓑ Ⓒ Ⓓ
4. Ⓐ Ⓑ Ⓒ Ⓓ
5. Ⓐ Ⓑ Ⓒ Ⓓ
6. Respond in booklet.

**Section B**

1. Ⓐ Ⓑ Ⓒ Ⓓ
2. Ⓐ Ⓑ Ⓒ Ⓓ
3. Ⓐ Ⓑ Ⓒ Ⓓ
4. Ⓐ Ⓑ Ⓒ Ⓓ
5. Ⓐ Ⓑ Ⓒ Ⓓ

**Section C**

1. Ⓐ Ⓑ Ⓒ Ⓓ
2. Ⓐ Ⓑ Ⓒ Ⓓ
3. Ⓐ Ⓑ Ⓒ Ⓓ
4. Ⓐ Ⓑ Ⓒ Ⓓ
5. Ⓐ Ⓑ Ⓒ Ⓓ
6. Ⓐ Ⓑ Ⓒ Ⓓ
7. Respond in booklet.

**Section D**

1. Respond in booklet.

**Section E**

1. Respond in booklet.

**Section F**

1. Ⓐ Ⓑ Ⓒ Ⓓ
2. Ⓐ Ⓑ Ⓒ Ⓓ
3. Ⓐ Ⓑ Ⓒ Ⓓ
4. Ⓐ Ⓑ Ⓒ Ⓓ
5. Ⓐ Ⓑ Ⓒ Ⓓ
6. Ⓐ Ⓑ Ⓒ Ⓓ
7. Respond in booklet.

**End of *Booklet 1***

---

### *BOOKLET 2*

**Section G**

1. Respond in booklet.

**Section H**

1. Ⓐ Ⓑ Ⓒ Ⓓ
2. Ⓐ Ⓑ Ⓒ Ⓓ
3. Ⓐ Ⓑ Ⓒ Ⓓ
4. Ⓐ Ⓑ Ⓒ Ⓓ

**Section I**

1. Ⓐ Ⓑ Ⓒ Ⓓ
2. Ⓐ Ⓑ Ⓒ Ⓓ
3. Ⓐ Ⓑ Ⓒ Ⓓ
4. Ⓐ Ⓑ Ⓒ Ⓓ
5. Ⓐ Ⓑ Ⓒ Ⓓ
6. Ⓐ Ⓑ Ⓒ Ⓓ
7. Ⓐ Ⓑ Ⓒ Ⓓ
8. Ⓐ Ⓑ Ⓒ Ⓓ
9. Ⓐ Ⓑ Ⓒ Ⓓ

**Section J**

1. Ⓐ Ⓑ Ⓒ Ⓓ
2. Ⓐ Ⓑ Ⓒ Ⓓ
3. Ⓐ Ⓑ Ⓒ Ⓓ
4. Ⓐ Ⓑ Ⓒ Ⓓ
5. Ⓐ Ⓑ Ⓒ Ⓓ
6. Respond in booklet.
7. Respond in booklet.

**Section K**

1. Respond in booklet.

**Section L**

1. Ⓐ Ⓑ Ⓒ Ⓓ
2. Ⓐ Ⓑ Ⓒ Ⓓ
3. Ⓐ Ⓑ Ⓒ Ⓓ
4. Ⓐ Ⓑ Ⓒ Ⓓ
5. Ⓐ Ⓑ Ⓒ Ⓓ
6. Ⓐ Ⓑ Ⓒ Ⓓ

---

### Student Questionnaire

**Section M**

1. Ⓨ Ⓝ
2. Ⓨ Ⓝ
3. Ⓨ Ⓝ
4. Ⓨ Ⓝ
5. Ⓨ Ⓝ
6. Ⓨ Ⓝ
7. Ⓨ Ⓝ
8. Ⓨ Ⓝ
9. Ⓨ Ⓝ

**End of Test**

---

Print Student Name: _____

_____

Student Signature: _____

# Writing a News Report

| Code | Descriptor |
|---|---|
| **Blank** | The pages are blank with nothing written or drawn in the space provided. |
| **Illegible** | The response is illegible, or irrelevant to the prompt. |
| **Off topic** | The response is off topic. |
| **Code 10** | The response is related to the headline and/or photo but is not a news report. **OR** The response is a news report related to the headline and/or photo. It identifies an event, but provides no supporting details, or provides details that are unrelated to the event. There is no evidence of organization. |
| **Code 20** | The response is related to the headline and/or photo but only partly in the form of a news report. **OR** The response is a news report related to the headline and/or photo, but the focus on an event is unclear or inconsistent. There is insufficient supporting details: too few or repetitious. There is limited evidence of organization. |
| **Code 30** | The response is a news report related to the headline and photo with a clear focus on the event. There are insufficient and/or vague supporting details or the connection of the details to the event is not always clear. There is evidence of organization, but lapses distract from the overall communication. |
| **Code 40** | The response is a news report related to the headline and photo with a clear and consistent focus on the event. There are sufficient supporting details, however, only some are specific. The organization is mechanical and any lapses do not distract from the overall communication. |
| **Code 50** | The response is a news report related to the headline and photo with a clear and consistent focus on the event. There are sufficient specific supporting details to develop the news report. The organization is logical. |
| **Code 60** | The response is a news report related to the headline and photo with a clear and consistent focus on an event. There are sufficient specific supporting details, which are thoughtfully chosen to develop the news report. The organization is coherent demonstrating a thoughtful progression of ideas. |

# News Report Conventions

| Code | Descriptor |
|------|------------|
| **Code 10** | There is insufficient evidence to assess the use of conventions.<br>**OR**<br>Errors in conventions interfere with communication. |
| **Code 20** | Errors in conventions distract from communication. |
| **Code 30** | Errors in conventions do not distract from communication. |
| **Code 40** | Control of conventions is evident in written work. |

# Long-Writing Topic Development

| Code | Descriptor |
|------|------------|
| **Blank** | The pages are blank with nothing written or drawn in the space provided. |
| **Illegible** | The response is illegible, or irrelevant to the prompt. |
| **Off topic** | The response is off topic. |
| **Code 10** | The response is related to the prompt but does not express an opinion.<br>**OR**<br>The response expresses an opinion with no supporting details or provides details unrelated to the opinion. There is no evidence of organization. |
| **Code 20** | The response is related to the prompt, but only part of the response expresses and supports an opinion.<br>**OR**<br>The response is related to the prompt, and expresses and supports an opinion, but the opinion is unclear or inconsistent. There are insufficient supporting details: too few or repetitious. There is limited evidence of organization. |
| **Code 30** | The response is related to the prompt and expresses a clear opinion. There are insufficient and/or vague supporting details or the connection of the details to the opinion is not always clear. There is evidence of organization, but lapses distract from the overall communication. |
| **Code 40** | The response is related to the prompt. A clear and consistent opinion is developed with sufficient supporting details, however only some are specific. The organization is mechanical and any lapses do not distract from the overall communication. |
| **Code 50** | The response is related to the prompt. A clear and consistent opinion is developed with sufficient specific supporting details. The organization is logical. |
| **Code 60** | The response is related to the assigned prompt. A clear and consistent opinion is developed with sufficient specific supporting details that are thoughtfully chosen. The organization is coherent demonstrating a thoughtful progression of ideas. |

**STUDENT HANDOUT FOR *THE OSSLT LITERACY LAB***

# Long-Writing Conventions

| Code | Descriptor |
|---|---|
| **Code 10** | There is insufficient evidence to assess the use of conventions. **OR** Errors in conventions interfere with communication. |
| **Code 20** | Errors in conventions distract from communication. |
| **Code 30** | Errors in conventions do not distract from communication. |
| **Code 40** | Control of conventions is evident in written work. |

# Open-Response

| Code | Descriptor |
|---|---|
| Blank | **nothing written or drawn in the space provided** |
| Illegible | **response is illegible or is a comment on the task (e.g., I don't know.)** |
| Off topic/ Incorrect | **response is off-topic, irrelevant or incorrect**<br><br>a typical off-topic response provides no information from the reading selection.<br><br>A typical irrelevant response comments on the reading selection or simply restates the question.<br><br>A typical incorrect response<br>    - provides an answer based on a misunderstanding of the question<br>      AND/OR the ideas in the reading selection.<br>**OR**<br>    - provides a general comment about the selection. |
| Code 10 | • **response indicates minimal reading comprehension**<br>• **response provides minimal or irrelevant ideas and information from the reading selection**<br><br>The response provides information with<br>    - no support or details from the selection<br>**OR**<br>    - a retelling of events in the reading selection<br>**OR**<br>    - irrelevant details from the selection |
| Code 20 | • **response indicates some reading comprehension**<br>• **response provides vague ideas and information from the reading selection; it may include irrelevant ideas and information from the reading selection**<br><br>The response provides a response with a vague explanation. The response often requires the reader to make connections. |
| Code 30 | • **response indicates considerable reading comprehension**<br>• **response provides accurate, specific and relevant ideas and information from the reading selection** |

# Short-Writing Task

| Code | Descriptor |
|---|---|
| Blank | nothing written or drawn in the space provided |
| Illegible | response is illegible or is a comment on the task (e.g., I don't know.) |
| Off topic/ Incorrect | response is off-topic, irrelevant or incorrect<br><br>A typical off-topic response is not related to the topic.<br><br>A typical irrelevant response comments on the topic or simply restates the questions. |
| Code 10 | response is not developed or is developed with irrelevant ideas and information |
| Code 20 | response is developed with vague ideas and information; it may contain some irrelevant ideas and information |
| Code 30 | response is developed with clear, specific and relevant ideas and information |

# Last Minute Advice

- make sure you know the location of where you will be writing the test ahead of time
- get a good night's sleep before the test
- double-check your alarm
- eat a good breakfast
- make sure you have pencils or pens (blue or black ink only)
- **don't leave any blanks**; partial marks are better than no marks
- check your work for organization, clarity, spelling and grammar
- budget your time
- fill the space provided
- use formal language
- use complete sentences
- stay calm and collected

**STUDENT HANDOUT FOR *THE OSSLT LITERACY LAB***

# Quotes

"Learning is not a spectator sport.
-D. Blocher

"It is wiser to find out than to suppose."
- Mark Twain

"Even if you're on the right track,
you'll get run over if you just sit there."
-Will Rogers

"Learning is like rowing upstream,
not to advance is to drop back."
- Proverb

"Be a student as long as you still have something to learn,
and this will mean all your life."
- Henry L. Doherty

"Just believe in yourself.
Even if you don't, pretend that you do and, at some point you will."
-Venus Williams

"The expert in anything was once a beginner."
-Unknown

"Every single thing that you learn really just gives you more comfort.
It's something I counsel kids all the time: if someone is willing to
teach you something for free, take them up on it.
Do it. Every single time. All it does is make you more likely to be able
to succeed. And it's kind of a nice way to go through life."
- Chris Hadfield

# Connect

| | |
|---|---|
| EQAO | eqao.com |
| Wintertickle Press | winterticklepress.com |
| OSSLT Literacy Lab | OSSLTliteracylab.com |
| Facebook–Wintertickle Press | facebook.com/winterticklepress |
| Facebook–OSSLT Literacy Lab | facebook.com/OSSLTliteracylab |
| Twitter–Wintertickle Press | @wintertickle |
| Email | ontarioliteracylab@outlook.com |
| Phone | 1-800-810-9845 |
| Fax | 1-866-580-1042 |
| Mailing Address | 132 Commerce Park Drive, Unit K, Suite 155, Barrie, ON, L4N 0Z7 |

# Also Available

Check out our non-printable PDF file of *The OSSLT Literacy Lab*, perfect for use with SMART Board® technology. For more information, visit www.winticklepress.com.

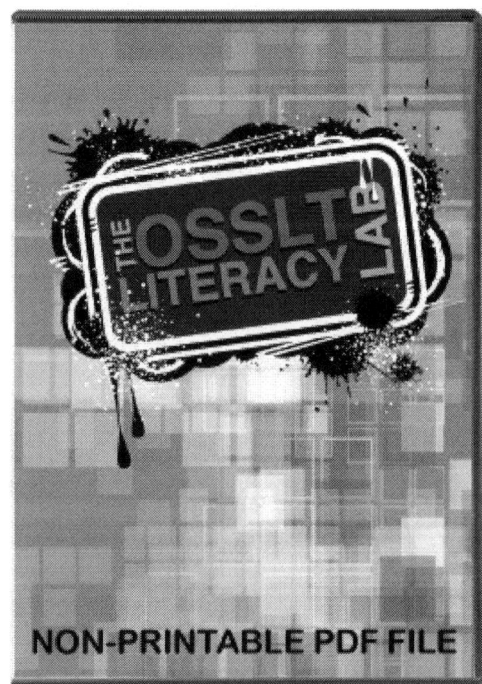

THE OSSLT LITERACY LAB

NON-PRINTABLE PDF FILE

61047400R00076